W9-AKS-760

When God
Doesn't
Heal Now

When God

Doesn't

Heal Now

How to Walk by Faith Facing Pain,
Suffering, and Death

Larry Keefauver, D.Min.

THOMAS NELSON PUBLISHERS®
Nashville

Copyright © 2000 by Larry Keefauver

All rights reserved. Written permission must be secured from the publisher to use or reproduce any part of this book, except for brief quotations in critical reviews or articles.

Published in Nashville, Tennessee, by Thomas Nelson, Inc.

Unless otherwise noted, Scripture quotations are from THE NEW KING JAMES VERSION. Copyright © 1979, 1980, 1982, Thomas Nelson, Inc., Publishers.

Scripture quotations noted KJV are from THE KING JAMES VERSION.

Scripture quotations noted NIV are from the HOLY BIBLE: NEW INTERNATIONAL VERSION®. Copyright © 1973, 1978, 1984 by International Bible Society. Used by permission of Zondervan Publishing House. All rights reserved.

Scripture quotations noted NLT are from the *Holy Bible,* New Living Translation, copyright © 1996. Used by permission of Tyndale House Publishers, Inc., Wheaton, Illinois 60189. All rights reserved.

Library of Congress Cataloging-in-Publication Data

Keefauver, Larry.
    When God doesn't heal now : how to walk by faith, facing pain, suffering, and death / Larry Keefauver.
        p. cm.
    ISBN 0-7852-6975-4 (pbk.)
    1. Spiritual healing. I. Title.
BT732.5.K44 2000
234'.131—dc21   99-34137
                                                            CIP

Printed in the United States of America

1 2 3 4 5 6 QPV 05 04 03 02 01 00

This book is dedicated to the memory of
Carol Gorrel,
whose walk of faith in pain, suffering, and death
prompted this writing.
To Tom and Deanna Freiling,
whose faith and courage were a light in darkness.

"For to me, to live is Christ, and to die is gain."
—Philippians 1:21

CONTENTS

ACKNOWLEDGMENTS

I give thanks to Christ
for the wonderful support for the project given by
Mike Hyatt, Cindy Blades,
and Brian Hampton at Thomas Nelson;
for my wife, Judi;
for my pastor, Sam Hinn;
for my congregation and YMCS partners;
for my dear friends—Lynn Gorrel, Lisa Burleson,
and Tom Freiling.

We have seen that God's healing ministry is rooted in his eternal desire to glorify himself and his Son, his deep compassion for those who are suffering, and his constant willingness to respond to those who have faith. He also heals in response to his own command and promise to the church. These four reasons alone ought to convince us that God's purposes for healing are rooted in his unchanging nature, not in temporary historical circumstances.

Yet the Scriptures give other reasons why God heals . . . He heals to lead people to repentance and open doors for the gospel. He heals to remove hindrances to ministry and service. He heals to teach us about himself and his kingdom. He heals to demonstrate the presence of the kingdom. He heals simply because people ask him. And he heals for sovereign purposes known only to himself. None of these reasons is based on the changing historical circumstances of the first-century church. They are rooted in the character and eternal purposes of God.

—JACK DEERE,
Surprised by the Power of the Spirit

WHEN THE GOD WHO HEALS DOESN'T HEAL NOW

Don't read further, unless you have questions about your healing. If you have all the answers you need and have *never* wondered why the God who Heals doesn't always heal *now*, then you have no need for this book.

Because this book is for those who have . . .

- believed God for their healing but nothing's happened . . . yet.

- prayed for their healing but have not yet seen an answer.

- confessed every known promise and word about healing in God's Word, but still their healing tarries.

- repented of all past sins of omission and commission and still not been healed.

- wondered why the God who Heals doesn't heal them *now*.

Perhaps you are the one who is ill, and though you have cried out day and night from your sickbed, God seems more distant now than ever before. King David found himself in such a place: "I am poured out like water, / And all My bones are out of joint; / My heart is like wax; / It has melted within Me. / My strength is dried up like a potsherd, / And My tongue clings to My jaws; / You have brought Me to the dust of death" (Ps. 22:14–15). So you ask, "Why has God brought me here?" And even more disturbing, "Why has God left me here—in the pit of sickness?"

So your pain unceasingly drills deep into your body and soul until you would rather die than go on, but God has not yet answered nor has He taken the pain away. Or your faith, which once was strong, confident, and vibrant, now wanes with the stress of hurting and the doubts of endless hours passing without relief from pain.

You may be the one who is sick. Or a loved one—a family member, spouse, parent, child, or friend—may be wasting away before your eyes as you vainly try to stem the relentless waves of despair, hopelessness, and discouragement that pound the shoreline of your faith more intensely with each passing day.

If building a bridge of faith seems impossible . . .

If praying for healing feels hopeless . . .

If believing one more promise stretches you beyond the breaking point . . .

Then, this book is for you.

YOU CAN WALK BY FAITH

When God doesn't heal now, it is still possible to walk by faith through pain, through suffering, and even while facing death. What will cripple your walk and sabotage your faith is believing myths about healing that on the surface sound so comforting and reassuring, but when put to the test leave you empty and dry.

The myths about healing and faith sounded so real when you or the one you loved was well. It was easy to sing and shout clichés when all was well with your soul. But months and even years of disease can peel back the facade of trite religion and expose the shallowness of quick-fix religious language. And when the early stages of your illness passed and healing did not come, you found yourself face-to-face with your own imminent mortality. Beneath your feet was a quicksand of myths that no longer supported your pain-filled days and sleepless nights. Now where do you turn for rock-solid truth that will see you through even the "valley of the shadow of death"?

What are some of the myths we banter about when talk is cheap and life seems endless? Here are a few:

- If a person has enough faith, they will be healed.
- God answers every prayer for healing prayed in faith.
- Past or unconfessed sin hinders or blocks one's healing.
- Not being healed indicates God's punishment or judgment.
- If one who is sick can just be prayed for by certain healing evangelists or preachers, then they will be healed.
- When God doesn't heal now, just wait. Your healing is coming.
- Doubt stops God's healing power.
- Healing can only occur in the right atmosphere of worship.

- Those who are healed are blessed. Those not healed are cursed.

- Sick people must never speak of their illness.

When I call such statements "myths," I am not suggesting that they are devoid of truth. They may have been derived from actual experiences or even surmised from biblical texts. I am using this definition of *myth* for our discussion:

> *A myth may be a story which is present in terms of some symbolism and thus has a poetic or emotional appeal and is capable of reinterpretation in the light of fresh experiences. Some of the deepest feelings of people about the human predicament may find expression in mythical form.*[1]

In fact, what makes these myths so appealing and even addictive in their use in various preaching and teaching circles is that they do have some basis in fact, are rooted in deep emotions, and find some support in Scripture. But like an onion, when all the layers of experience and proclamation are peeled away, nothing of lasting substance remains at the core of a myth.

A myth serves us well for a time or a season or even an experience. But myths cannot stand the test of truth. Truth is that which is true for all time, for all people, and in all situations. A myth only seems true for some times, for some people, and in some situations.

It has been easier for you to believe what some preacher, teacher, or evangelist has told you about healing than to grapple with what God says. It has been more expedient to pray the way others pray than to cry out with the deep groaning of the Spirit welling up from the recesses of your spirit and soul.

Before now, few have told you that sickness really hurts . . . that pain often doesn't go away with either a word or a pill . . . and that suffering is rarely glorious and too often simply tears deeply into the fabric of hope. You may now be asking these questions:

- If God has healed me by the stripes of Jesus, then why haven't I been healed?

- If God's will is for all to be healed, then when will I be a part of the "all"?

- If healing is my right to claim, then why can't I claim it now?

Don't feel guilty for asking your questions. Refuse to be silenced in your anguish. Know that your questions will not put you outside the realm of faith nor will they keep you from being healed. In truth, walking by faith is much more difficult than talking about faith. Talk is cheap until the moment a doctor says, "cancer" or "heart disease" or "kidney failure."

When faced with the reality of a life-threatening disease, we need more than myths. We need the truth of God's Word: "He sent His word and healed them, / And delivered them from their destructions" (Ps. 107:20).

Get ready. In the coming pages you will learn not just how to talk the walk of faith, but how to walk the talk. You will meet two families that faced terminal disease. One woman was healed in time while the other was healed in eternity. Both walked by faith. Their courage, faith, hope, and spiritual depth will help you in your journey of faith to know the God who Heals!

I've had people say to me, "Well, if you believe in divine healing, then that means you believe people will never die." No, because the Bible says it is appointed unto men once to die. There is an appointment with death for each person who is not raptured. Just don't leave too soon because of sickness.

In Matthew 9:29, Jesus said, . . . According to your faith let it be to you. If it's according to your faith concerning the healing of your body, then it could be according to your faith concerning your homegoing.

Your time for homegoing, like Paul's, should come only after you have Fought a good fight . . . finished your course . . . kept the faith (2 Tim. 4:7 KJV).

—BILLY JOE DAUGHERTY,
You Can Be Healed

CHAPTER 1

IS IT *WHY* OR *WHEN* GOD DOESN'T HEAL?

Years ago, we organized an exciting trip from west Texas to Oklahoma City. Benny Hinn was conducting a healing crusade in Oklahoma City just a few weeks after the federal building had been bombed. A busload of hopeful believers led a caravan of trucks and suburbans across those flat plains into a packed coliseum in the center of the city.

Our group waited hours in line as expectant crowds thronged the entrances. Many in wheelchairs, on crutches, led by Seeing Eye dogs, and even some on stretchers pushed their way forward as the doors opened into an arena transformed into a sanctuary. Everyone entered into a worship service that majestically ushered all of us into God's presence.

As we filed in, one woman rushed up to our group and excitedly joined her sister who had come with us. Barbara introduced her sister, Cindy, to me as we moved forward into the arena. Flushed with hope, Barbara said, "We are believing for Cindy's healing. We have prayed for months and confessed that she would be healed during this crusade. We know

1

God will heal her and many of her unsaved friends will see her miracle and be saved."

The layers of interwoven myths had been so reverently bound into the fabric of their faith that it would have been impossible to separate truth from myth or reality from perception. So important was her healing to her faith that if she didn't realize the former, then the latter was certainly to shatter.

Inside the great hall, the crowd's expectancy was so intense that some were being healed long before the service commenced. Others would rush forward toward the altar professing their healing as the worship and singing moved from exuberant praise to whispered reverence.

Then as Benny Hinn spoke words of knowledge the arena seemed to rivet with lightning bolts of power as people from every corner rushed forward to ascend the platform stairs and testify to God's healing miracles in their lives.

After the first night's service, the sick sister, Cindy, remained physically infirm. However, her faith seemed undaunted. She confessed that God was only testing her by making her wait on her healing one more night and that the devil was barraging her with weapons of doubt. But *no weapon formed against her would prosper.* Hence, the next night, she believed, would be the nexus of faith, power, and prayer all culminating in her healing.

For those not healed on Thursday evening, the mounting pressure of expecting a healing on Friday so increased that it felt like a volcano of spiritual power and resurrection dynamism could explode at any moment during the Friday night service. And explode it did. Thousands rushed forward to be saved at an altar call. Thousands more shouted praise as they experienced God's healing power during the service.

Hundreds filled the aisles leading to the altars. All in line hoped for the opportunity to testify to the Spirit and fall under the Spirit's power as Benny prayed for them.

But Cindy wasn't among the thousands who were saved or healed *now!* And like every other mountaintop experience that comes to an end—including the Old Testament account of defeating the prophets of Baal on Mt. Carmel and the New Testament narrative of Jesus on the mount being transfigured with Moses and Elijah—this God encounter likewise descended the steep slopes of glory into the mundane routine of everyday life. For Cindy, going back to life as usual without being physically healed by God was totally unacceptable.

"Take me up on the platform," she insisted. "Get Benny to pray for me."

Of course, as Benny has continually asserted through the years, he has never healed anyone. Only God heals. The great healing evangelists have all insisted that they don't heal—Wigglesworth, Lake, Woodworth-Etter, Kuhlman, Roberts, and many others through the decades have proclaimed God as the Healer and no other.

Cindy's facade of faith crumpled, and her veneer of piety fractured under the pressure of her very real predicament. She must go home and back to work facing all those people to whom she had predicted her imminent healing. Out of her heart, Cindy spoke. She bitterly denounced Benny Hinn, all healing evangelists, all preachers, all those around her, and finally, with acid bitterness, she denounced God. All had failed her, and she left the arena sick, broken, and faithless.

As she angrily walked out, her last question, spoken more as an epithet than a query, spit from her mouth like a viper's venom and echoed hollowly through the bystanders around her: "Why didn't God heal me tonight? He promised!" Deserted by her myths, she left empty and tragically alone.

"WHEN" NEEDS A COMPLETION

Many preachers, theologians, and televangelists address the question "Why doesn't God heal now?" Their answers often must be anchored in myth because Scripture simply doesn't answer the question with a neat one-line sound bite. Such a question squirms out of the same can of worms as "Why does a good and loving God allow suffering?" Volumes have been written trying to pen the biblical answer to the problem of suffering, but no one answer fully lights every dark corner of this shadowy perplexity.

When God doesn't heal now truthfully can never be posed as a question because it's simply a dangling phrase begging for completion. No myth can complete the sentence, finalize the phrase, or give meaning to a life threatened by disease and death.

Sadly, too many people—preachers and theologians alike—have tried to use myths to comfort those who have traveled for miles and stood for hours to get into a healing crusade, stood in a healing line, and even been prayed for by a sincere usher, altar worker, or healing evangelist only to return home still sick and hurting—physically, emotionally, and spiritually. Who writes the books for them? Who tells their stories as they battle chemotherapy, languish in hospital rooms, or lie lonely and unhealed in their bedrooms at home?

Yes, excitement and hope electrify live crowds and television viewers when a terminally ill believer testifies to a good report of being healed instantly. But no camera or reporter follows the scores of sick people who file silently away from the altar or travel for hours to go back home after not being healed now in a healing service or prayer line. For them, myths of healing only deepen their pain, exacerbate their guilt, and erode their hope and faith.

The God who Heals never intended for us to contrive shallow answers to deep questions. Nor does He need our help in defending Him or His self-appointed spokespersons in explaining why people are not healed now. As I suggested earlier, a myth is something that is rooted in the experience of some and then masquerades as truth for all.

You may have found yourself exercising great faith, anchored in indefatigable hope, while believing and confessing your healing or healing for another only to be left waiting, wondering, and asking yourself, "What now, Lord?"

I recently heard an itinerant prophet confess that her father was dying. Loudly and boldly she would visit him in his nursing home room, declaring his healing and giving God praise. "As long as there is breath in him, I will hope for a miracle," she proclaimed. Her words inspired me. Her faith edified me. And her courage filled me with admiration. But she also confessed to the pain and anguish of seeing her father slowly waste away with a terminal disease. She shared how she would sing old choruses they both loved as she held his hand.

"Peace would fill his room," she confided. Perhaps her touch and her compassionate songs came closer to completing the sentence "When God doesn't heal now . . ." than to answering all the *why* questions.

IT'S MORE THAN *WHY?*—IT'S *WHEN*

The *why* questions boggle the mind and drown the heart in mystery.

- If we have been healed by His stripes (Isa. 53:5), then *why* aren't all believers healed?

- *Why* did all those whom Jesus healed die?

- *Why* is it that some who have great faith are healed and some are not?

- *Why* does God choose to heal those who have no faith while some godly saints go unhealed?

These are just a few of the questions. Even asking all the *why* questions is as hopeless a task as finding a completely satisfying answer to even one of them. Myths about healing mix some related Scriptures, with some personal experiences and testimonies about healing and then proffer doctrines that supposedly comfort both the sick and those grieving for the dead.

God in His profound wisdom has sent forth healing by His Word (not myth) not only to heal the sick but also to mend broken hearts, comfort those mourning, and sustain the dying. The good news is not just for *those healed now* but also for *those not healed now*. God's Spirit ministers to both the person healed temporally and the one healed eternally. In fact, the greatest healing miracle of all is not the *one* healed now . . . but the one *saved* now!

If you are sick or praying for someone who is sick, this book is for you. God may physically heal you or them at any moment, or He may heal you or them eternally on the other side of death. One thing is certain. Between now and eternity, time will pass. How you spend that precious commodity will result in either treasure or trash. That time will be either redeemed or wasted. The choice is yours.

Until your healing is manifested either in time or eternity, you will either walk by faith or merely talk faith. Walking by faith is really living, whether for a moment longer or for years. Talking faith will only spin the dream weaver's web of myths that will leave both you and those around you discouraged, disheartened, angry, resentful, and bitter.

When God doesn't heal you now, you may be tempted to diminish your trust and increase your trying. At times, you may become so desperate you will try anything in the natural or spiritual just to force the hand of God.

You may chase after exotic medical treatments or New Age philosophies. You may find yourself believing the advice of anyone or any book that addresses your problem. You may even build altars to the world's gurus who promise quick fixes for big bucks.

I want to encourage you to walk by faith in Christ your Healer, not in the religious clichés or the worldly quick fixes that are proffered. Your trying will not get you healed. You can be bold and assertive in your faith, in your prayers, and in wielding God's sword, His Word, as you fight violently against every attack of the enemy on your body and soul. But you cannot make a miracle happen. Some will advise you to expect a miracle. Actually you can do better than that. You can expect God to meet you at your point of need and walk with you every moment of life. Don't be discouraged. When all the platitudes fail and the quick fixes fade, Christ remains at your side to lift you up and see you through.

When God doesn't heal you *now,* you can walk by faith through any pain, suffering, or valley of the shadow of death. Here's how.

TWO HEALINGS—ONE IN TIME; ONE IN ETERNITY

In the coming pages, you will read the story of two women. Joani suddenly and without warning went into systemic organ failure. For months, she was kept alive only by machines. Her brain wave was flat. Doctors believed her to be brain-dead and counseled Rob, her husband, to pull the plug. He walked by faith, refused to give up, and witnessed Joani's miraculous and complete physical healing.

Alicia heard the shocking news and left the doctor's office feeling completely numb. She had liver cancer. Only a tiny percentage live more than a few months with Alicia's type of liver disease, Alicia learned from her doctor.

Once the shock wore off, Alicia and her husband, William, determined to walk by faith. They prayed powerfully and effectively. They confessed the Word and experienced the faithful prayer support of believing family, friends, and their church. While their faith increased and grew even through arduous trials, Alicia's condition steadily worsened. She consulted with outstanding Christian physicians and went whenever possible to worship services. Elders prayed and anointed her with oil. Still, she grew physically weaker until finally she died. Nonetheless, she was healed in eternity and finished strong walking by faith in Jesus Christ.

In both stories, God moved in miraculous and mighty ways. Healing myths would dictate that Rob and Joani had victorious faith while William's and Alicia's faith was defeated. The truth is that William's and Alicia's faith was just as real and effective even though God did not heal *now*.

First, we will hear the stories. Then we will peel away the myths. Finally, we will learn how to walk by faith through pain, suffering, and even death.

Physical healings are exhilarating.
They stir up your faith in God and they draw people to Jesus.
Yet there is a healing that is greater.
I'm talking about the healing of your spirit—THE REAL YOU.
The spiritual healing I am speaking about IS ETERNAL.
While physical healing benefits you greatly in this life,
Spiritual healing has benefits NOW and in ETERNITY.

—PETER YOUNGREN,
A Study of God the Healer

CHAPTER 2

HEALING IN TIME
AND ETERNITY

God heals both in time and eternity. As the God who acts in history, God declared and demonstrated Himself as *Yahweh-Rapha'*, the "LORD who heals" (Ex. 15:26). *When* healing will be manifested has always been a concern to those suffering from disease. The natural desire is for healing *now*—in time and space. That God heals as a wondrous sign in history is truth. That God must always heal *now* because we believe, obey, or confess the Word is myth. The myths will be handled later.

At the end of Chapter 1, I introduced you to two remarkable families—Rob and Joani; William and Alicia. The names have been changed, but the stories are true. Both couples with their families faced life-threatening illness. Both couples responded in faith, obeyed God's Word, and confessed that God heals. Joani was miraculously healed physically in time; Alicia was miraculously healed physically in eternity. Joani's present dwelling place is a physical body; Alicia is at home with the Lord. One of their stories could well be yours. Both couples attended the same church and believed unswervingly that God is the God who Heals.

HEALED IN TIME AND SPACE

Francis Schaeffer correctly observed that God as revealed in Scripture is a personal-infinite God who acts both in eternity and in time and space.[1] Paul R. House wrote that biblical canon "defines the Lord by character traits and by deeds accomplished."[2] J. N. Scofield wrote that the God of the Old Testament is "the almighty God who is always, everywhere, lovingly active."[3] The stage of God's word and actions is history, and we are the audience. Through the eyes and words of Moses, David, Isaiah, Ezekiel, Peter, Paul, and a multitude of others, God has revealed Himself to us in Spirit-breathed Scripture. One absolute truth revealed by both word and act in Scripture, simply put, is this: *God heals.* He has healed, is healing, and will heal.

In the Torah, God revealed, "If you diligently heed the voice of the LORD your God and do what is right in His sight, give ear to His commandments and keep all His statutes, I will put none of the diseases on you which I have brought on the Egyptians. For I am the LORD who heals you" (Ex. 15:26). And in the new covenant, Jesus declared, "The Spirit of the LORD is upon Me, / Because He has anointed Me / To preach the gospel to the poor; / He has sent Me to heal the brokenhearted, / To proclaim liberty to the captives / And recovery of sight to the blind, / To set at liberty those who are oppressed" (Luke 4:18).

The same God who is there in the old and new covenants is the God of today—compassionately comforting and healing His people. Through the stripes of Jesus, those whose faith is in Him are saved and healed in time and for eternity.

> For to this you were called, because Christ also suffered for us, leaving us an example, that you should follow His steps: "Who committed no sin, / Nor was deceit found in His mouth"; who, when He was reviled, did not revile in return; when He suffered, He did not threaten, but committed Himself to Him who judges righteously; who Himself bore our sins in His own body on the tree, that we, having died to sins, might live for righteousness—by whose stripes you were healed. For you were like sheep going astray, but have now returned to the Shepherd and Overseer of your souls. (1 Peter 2:21–25)

The God who Heals miraculously healed Joani in time and space.

RESTORED FROM DEATH'S PRECIPICE

In August of 1986, Rob and Joani sold their business and home and moved to Florida. To them Florida was a land flowing with the milk and honey of opportunity. Filled with excitement and hope, they purchased a new home, started a business, and felt that they were putting down roots for the first time in years. To make things sweeter, Joani's family— her sister—lived just houses away. As young girls, the sisters had lost both their mother and father, so to each other, they were all the family they had in the world.

During this time, Rob and Joani's faith grew by leaps and bounds. Through Kenneth Copeland's ministry and other books and teachings, both had learned how to confess the promises and prosperity of God. The blessings of Deuteronomy 28 seemed to flow freely into their lives. God also gave them a word of knowledge in those years that He would fulfill their heart's desire for another child. A son had been born to them early in their marriage, but for years they were unable to have a second child. Now God had promised the long-awaited child.

Then less than a year later, in May of 1987, tragedy struck unexpectedly. Early that spring day, Rob left for work while Joani drove their son to school. Rushing back home to meet a furniture delivery truck, Joani felt a headache slowly penetrating her forehead. Sinus headache from allergies, she thought. The move to Florida had exposed her to new pollen and previously unencountered allergens that had recently caused watery eyes and a runny nose with a scratchy throat.

God was blessing those things that Rob and Joani did. It was exciting for them to see their business and personal lives prosper. Up to this time, they had never experienced any major sicknesses or health problems. God had met all of their needs including the desire of their hearts to live in Florida. So thinking that her headache was simply a minor irritation in an otherwise sunny day and wonderful life, Joani ignored the headache pressure and continued with her busy day.

The persistent ache, however, didn't lessen. In fact, as she picked her son up from school and returned home to cook dinner, she felt worse. When Rob arrived home from work, Joani confessed, "Rob, my head is really bothering me. I've got this nasty headache. So I'm going to lie down for a while." Rob laid hands on her head, rebuked the headache, and then Joani lay down to sleep.

Right before 2:00 A.M. Joani awoke with an excruciating pain throbbing in her head. Hurting and disoriented, Joani woke Rob, saying, "Something is wrong. I think you need to get me to the hospital." Rob called Joani's sister for help and then proceeded to help Joani down the stairs of their two-story home. As she went through the downstairs, Joani felt a dark, ominous spirit approach her. A chill came over her as the spirit of death moved across the floor and penetrated her feet. From her toes through her legs and into her whole body, death moved in and life ebbed away. She cried out, "Rob, I'm dying!"

Jesus warned in John 10:10 that the enemy comes to kill and destroy: "The thief comes only to steal and kill and destroy; I have come that they may have life, and have it to the full" (NIV). Joani felt death's grip on her life as a dark curtain fell over her consciousness and her life precariously hung by a thread of faith as Rob declared, "In the name of Jesus you are not dying. You are going to live."

Rushing Joani to the hospital, Rob and Joani's sister prayed militantly as Joani fought for her life. In the emergency room, the doctors and nurses worked intensely to keep Joani alive as they probed and ran tests for any clue to her sudden illness. Fearing she may have contracted a contagious disease, they moved her to isolation and made everyone who came near her wear sterile gowns and masks. Joani's vital signs continued to deteriorate. The doctors instructed Rob to call in family. "She's dying, and we don't know why," they solemnly admitted.

Like a drowning swimmer desperately breaking the water's surface to gasp for air, Joani swam between semiconsciousness and the dark, murky waters of unconsciousness.

Whenever she surfaced, she gave instructions to her family about her funeral and expressed her last wishes. Not allowing her instructions to dampen the atmosphere of faith and hope that Rob prayed into the room, he firmly spoke to his wife, "Joani, you are not going to die, but you are going to live." It seemed that Rob was alone in his confidence. Everyone, including Joani, prepared for the worst.

Joani's son approached her bedside and said, "Mama, you can't die because God's promise has not been fulfilled in your life." He reminded her of God's promise for another child. On different occasions and through different prophetic words, Joani and Rob had been promised another child. Surely God would not annul His promise. As her son spoke the promise, Joani reminded herself through the fog of ebbing consciousness, "God is not a man, that He should lie" (Num. 23:19).

The promise to Mary, which Joani had memorized, filled her mind: "Blessed is she who has believed that what the Lord has said to her will be accomplished" (Luke 1:45 NIV). Joani prayed, "Lord, this promise has not yet been performed in my life so I have got to live." As the cold darkness of coma enveloped her brain, Joani slipped into what would evolve into months upon months of a comatose state.

As she slipped into a coma, the doctor pronounced a death sentence: "The only thing I can say is we'll probably have a diagnosis within the next three days when we perform her autopsy because your wife will not live through the next seventy-two hours."

Rob immediately asked the doctor to leave Joani's room as he emphatically demanded, "I know you are telling me the facts, but there is a truth greater than your facts. If you have anything to tell me about Joani's condition, I would appreciate that you not tell me in the room with her. I do not want death spoken in her room."

Rob then confronted the doctor and asked, "Do you believe in miracles?" And the doctor said, "Well, yes. But not in this case."

Rob rebutted, "Well, I believe in miracles, and I know the Miracle Worker, and He is going to heal and He is going to restore my wife." First Corinthians 2:5 says that "your faith should not be in the wisdom of men but in the power of God." And Rob decided that that was where his faith would stand. Through the prayers and petitions of many people and through the undying love and faith of her husband and family, God did restore and heal Joani. But a long, hard spiritual battle was fought.

For months, Rob, Joani's sister, and Rob's mother kept a twenty-four-hour-a-day vigil at Joani's bedside. Scripture and worship tapes were played unceasingly. The nurses would hear the music and Scripture and protest, "Why are you doing this? She doesn't hear this." Nonetheless, Rob persisted.

When people called on the phone to ask about her condition, Rob would say, "Oh, she's better today." Rob decided to see the things that were not and by faith to declare them to be. Some felt that Rob was in denial and even lying about his wife's condition.

Specialists were brought in on Joani's case from the Centers for Disease Control in Atlanta and from Johns Hopkins Hospital. But no one had an encouraging prognosis. Later Joani would share that she was strangely aware of everything going on around her even though she could not move or speak. She did feel and experience all the prayers for her healing—both those in the room and those prayed by friends hundreds of miles away. She often says in her testimony, "I would see the prayers for me like a sacrifice of praise going up to the Father on my behalf. It looked like a smoke, a sweet-smelling savor going up to heaven. The power of praise and the power of prayer are what moved the hand of God."

After six weeks in a central Florida hospital, Joani's doctors decided to move her to a medical school hospital in Gainesville. Daily the doctors and students would make their rounds and discuss Joani's unique case as they gathered around her bed. Rob would often leave Christian television programs playing on the TV screen for hours at a time.

One day just as Rob walked into the room, the head of neurology pointed at the television screen and said, "I don't care if Oral Roberts himself were to reach his hand through that television and touch this woman, she couldn't be healed." Rob retorted, "Oral Roberts is not going to heal her. God is."

At one point, the doctors decided to do a radical procedure of using a drug-induced coma to take Joani to a deeper state of coma for three days. Family was asked to leave since Joani would be attended by doctors and nurses every moment of the procedure.

After one day of being away from Joani, her sister decided to visit in spite of the doctor's instructions. What she witnessed was shocking. All the orifices in Joani's body had tubes protruding from them. Joani's body had swollen to three times her original size. Joani's sister began to scream and cry in disbelief. Her doctor rushed into the room and began shouting, "I've got to tell you. Her husband will not accept the facts. We have tried to talk to him, and he will not believe the situation.

But I'm here to tell you that your sister is not going to live. She is brain-dead. If by any miracle her vital organs should start functioning again and she would ever see the day when she would get off the machine, she'll only be a vegetable. Right now she is brain-dead, and basically there is no hope."

Driving back to Orlando, Joani's sister, Jan, began to cry out to God. Telling Rob what the doctor had said, he rushed back to the hospital, praying along the way, "God, please, please don't let her die because if she dies, then I'm going to have to go in there and pray for her resurrection and have You resurrect her." After three days of the therapy, Joani's condition began to improve, and the doctors recommended brain surgery to reduce the pressure in the cranial cavity. Rob asked, "Is that all the help you can offer Joani?"

One of the doctors said, "Yes."

Rob replied, "Well, I can't let you do it. I'm taking her home." And the doctor looked at him and said, "My only advice to you then is to put her in a nursing home and let her live out her days."

Rob and Jan took Joani home. Still in a coma, she weighed less than eighty pounds. For months, Rob and Jan cared for every need. Joani was like a baby, and they cared for her totally. Still, they refused to give up hope and continued to confess their faith that God would heal Joani.

After months, Joani slowly recovered consciousness. She began to crawl and speak like a baby. But at times, she would violently attack those around her and would have to be restrained. Still, Rob persisted in his loving care and unceasing prayer.

When Joani first came home, Rob would read the Bible to her. Now the endless days stretched into months. The stress and constant caring for Joani began to take their toll on Rob. He was so weary he could barely make it through the day. Joani's physical care consumed every waking moment. Rob was becoming too tired to pray, to believe, or to walk by faith. He even took Joani to Oral Robert's City of Faith Hospital in Tulsa, Oklahoma. There they restrained Joani in the psychiatric ward. Slowly she improved. She began to recognize friends and family. Joani also became more peaceful and didn't have to be restrained. Having received some rest and spiritual refreshing, Rob took Joani back to Florida and continued to care for her. As weeks stretched into months, Joani improved until she was completely healed! Today she is a beautiful, vivacious Christian woman giving her testimony of God's healing power to everyone she meets.

She has returned to Gainesville for her doctors to see her amazing recovery. The head of neurology began to weep when he saw her fully healed and confessed, "I'm sorry, but I'm seeing a miracle of God." He said, "I read these tests when you were in before. I did this test on you, and there was no brain activity. To see you now, I know it's nothing the doctors could have done—it's only God."

One more thing must be told. Seven years later to the day from the day in May of 1987 when she had almost died in that central Florida hospital, Joani gave birth to the son God had promised. God had physically healed Joani and fulfilled His promise to Rob and Joani in the birth of their second child.

CROSSING OVER DEATH'S PRECIPICE

For years, William and Alicia had believed in the God who Heals. Though Alicia had been through a number of car accidents that had left her with pain in her back from time to time, they had walked by faith, trusting God to keep both of them in perfect health. During the last few weeks of 1997, Alicia's back began to hurt with a constant pain. Then at the end of January in 1998, Alicia woke up and felt very fatigued. After William left for work, she went back to bed and slept the entire day. That night she said to William, "I've never, ever done that before."

For a month Alicia's back pain continued to worsen. Finally, she went to see a chiropractor. While his treatments helped to relieve the pain temporarily, Alicia continued to ache and tire easily. Finally, William took his wife to her internist. At first, he thought she might have gallstones, but a sonogram came back negative. Then they looked for a pinched nerve in her back, but X rays revealed nothing. Not knowing what to do to relieve her pain, Alicia's doctor ordered an MRI.

By this time, Alicia had become so weakened by pain that she could barely endure the MRI test. Finally, after three tor- turous hours of tests, she emerged exhausted. The tests revealed nothing.

The pain continued and increased. A series of CAT scans was conducted, and finally in late February, at the end of the last test, the doctors found a serious problem. Lesions were discovered in Alicia's liver. After a biopsy confirmed that small carcinomas were present throughout her liver, the doc- tors pronounced their ominous diagnosis to William in a phone call at work: "Your wife is in the advanced stages of liver disease. Often the most aggressive chemotherapy will not help, but it is her only hope."

William went home early from work to tell Alicia.

William gave Alicia the news, and, both numb with shock, they wept together for a few minutes. William then looked at Alicia and asked, "So whose report do we believe in—God's or the doctor's?"

Both knew Scripture and immediately turned to Isaiah 53:1–5:

> Who has believed our report?
> And to whom has the arm of the LORD been revealed?
> For He shall grow up before Him as a tender plant,
> And as a root out of dry ground.
> He has no form or comeliness;
> And when we see Him,
> There is no beauty that we should desire Him.
> He is despised and rejected by men,
> A Man of sorrows and acquainted with grief.
> And we hid, as it were, our faces from Him;
> He was despised, and we did not esteem Him.
> Surely He has borne our griefs
> And carried our sorrows;
> Yet we esteemed Him stricken,
> Smitten by God, and afflicted.
> But He was wounded for our transgressions,
> He was bruised for our iniquities;
> The chastisement for our peace was upon Him,
> And by His stripes we are healed.

Alicia began to ask, "Why me when I've been through so much? I've been through all these things; now why this, Lord? There's one thing, I said, I don't ever want to get—this. I don't want to have it."

In more than twenty years of walking with the Lord, Alicia and William had experienced many things in their own family and in ministering to others who had been sick. They knew the report in their hands was real, but they also knew the reality of God's presence and promises. His voice spoke to both of them in those first moments of sharing an anguishing report of cancer together. "I am God, and I have a plan for you," whispered God's voice.

They turned to the reality of Jeremiah 29:11–13: "'For I know the plans I have for you,' says the LORD. 'They are plans for good and not for disaster, to give you a future and a hope. In those days when you pray, I will listen. If you look for me in earnest, you will find me when you seek me'" (NLT).

William said to Alicia, "What have we been doing for the last twenty-two years anyway? We've had catastrophe after catastrophe after catastrophe, and He's held us up with His right hand. Now, you were in a car wreck, and you got hurt bad. You were in a lot of car wrecks and got hurt bad, but you are not dead. So what did He do? He spared your life. We don't know what He is going to do right now. But whom are we serving? Or what are we going to do with this thing? This thing is the worst of the worst that we have seen so far—but we understand what we understand about cancer. So, what are we going to do?" And they did exactly what they had done with every prior catastrophe they had faced—they decided to put their lives in the hands of God. At that moment, by faith William and Alicia entrusted themselves anew to God's care and direction.

Alicia's daughter, Sonya, came over to comfort her parents. She determined by faith that she would not cave in to doubt and fear. Instead she found herself putting on God's armor (Eph. 6) and said to herself and her parents, "God has a plan in all of this. I am ready for war. I'm not going to let go of Mom without a fight." In William and Alicia's living room that evening, a trio of faithful warriors determined to believe God, to trust His plan, and to battle the enemy's attack of disease. All three believed that chemotherapy was not part of God's plan. God, not chemotherapy, would be their source.

The doctors held out no hope of recovery from any treatment, only the possibility of lengthening Alicia's life a few months. William, Alicia, and Sonya were not content with the bad report of a life for a few months. They claimed a good report for a complete and miraculous healing.

Seeking God's direction and knowing the Scriptures, Alicia and William determined to walk by faith through this valley, one step at a time. First they called on their pastor and the elders to pray and anoint them with oil. "Are any among you sick? They should call for the elders of the church and have them pray over them, anointing them with oil in the name of the Lord. And their prayer offered in faith will heal the sick, and the Lord will make them well. And anyone who has committed sins will be forgiven" (James 5:14–15 NLT).

They read healing Scriptures daily. Their home was filled with Scripture choruses and worship-filled music. William and Alicia confessed her healing and continued to trust God's promises. They sought advice from a leading Christian doctor and physically built up Alicia's immune system through good nutrition and supplements. They even considered going to a clinic in Mexico for a period of time that promised therapy that would further strengthen Alicia's immune system. But after prayer with the elders and seeking God's will, they determined that the walk of faith they were following was to stay where they were and to continue to trust His leading.

For a few months, Alicia's condition improved. They fully believed that God was physically healing her.

Christian friends surrounded Alicia and William. Daily, friends from the church would visit them and pray with them. They also met Rob and Joani. Often, the two couples would spend an entire evening praying together and confessing God's healing promises.

At times, Alicia would want William to talk about the possibility that she might go to heaven. At first, William refused to talk about any possibility of death. But then he realized that the loving thing to do was to allow her to talk about all her feelings. Neither one had given up hope or had given in to a spirit of fear.

Sonya and her husband were also part of some family discussions that faced the possibility that Alicia might die and go home with the Lord. They claimed God's promise in 2 Timothy 1:7: "For God has not given us a spirit of fear and timidity, but of power, love, and self-discipline" (NLT). All confessed the healing power of God and trusted Him to care for them in His plan.

Daily Sonya would put her mom in God's hands. One day she asked herself, "Will you still love God if Mom isn't healed now?" Fighting back the tears, Sonya confessed her unending love for God and continued to believe that His plan was to heal her mom.

Daily William and Alicia would confess God's promises of healing. But by late spring, Alicia's pain had become intolerable. She received painkilling medication by IV and finally became so sick from the painkilling therapy that she was admitted into the hospital for a short period of time to be freed from the toxicity of the medication.

She grew stronger and returned home feeling much better. But the improvement was short-lived, and steadily she weakened. Problems arose continually with her IV therapy, but still the whole family walked in faith. For a few weeks, they all were able to go to worship services and be prayed for by the whole congregation. Everyone believed she would be physically healed *now!*

William and Alicia continually watched Christian TV, especially Benny Hinn and Richard and Lindsey Roberts. They confessed that Alicia was healed by the stripes of Jesus Christ. Alicia would try to eat solid food, but nausea kept her from desiring much food. The spiritual warfare intensified. Elders visited regularly to pray, give praise to God, worship with, and encourage the family.

June arrived with William and his son now taking shifts to care for Alicia. Her pain never ceased. Even with proper medication, she rarely felt relief. As she weakened, she insisted on talking with her family about what might happen if she went home to be with the Lord. As painful as those talks were, the love of God filled their home and comforted each family member.

As the hot, humid July days slowly passed in central Florida, William saw his wife's life ebbing away. He knew it was the eleventh hour, but he also knew that God could heal in the eleventh hour, that with God, nothing is impossible. William and Alicia expected God to heal and were at peace with God's sovereignty. Her life was in His hands. His plan and will would reign supreme in their lives. Nothing mattered but totally trusting God and walking by faith.

By mid-July, Alicia was gone. One morning, with William and Sonya at her side, she stepped over the precipice of death and entered eternal life—healed by His stripes.

THE PARADOX OF BEING HEALED NOW AND BEING HEALED ETERNALLY

Both couples walked by faith. In one instance, God healed physically in a miraculous way in time and space. In the other instance, God healed eternally. The greatest healing is salvation—not being cured physically. The greatest enemy is not death, but hell. Yet, some might feel that Joani *won* and Alicia *lost*.

How paradoxical it was that one couple, Rob and Joani, found themselves ministering to another couple, William and Alicia! What is a paradox? A paradox is when two seeming contradictions are truth when they are held together. Scripture is filled with paradoxes. The first must be last. The poor are truly rich. Leaders are servants, and those who gain their lives will lose them.

Healing is paradoxical truth. God heals both in time and in eternity. In fact, without being healed eternally, being healed in time is meaningless. Both couples approached the threat of death with faith. One wife was healed physically while the other wife died. Consider these questions:

- Did one couple do something right while the other couple tragically missed something?

- Did God will for one to be healed and one to die?

- Could it be that both couples walked by faith, and God's plan for each was different?

- In the battles that each couple fought, was healing the ultimate issue?

- Or was faith the ultimate issue?

- Or even more paradoxical for us to understand, was it the One in whom faith was placed?

The real spiritual battlefield on which we war against disease is not healing but faith. The paramount struggle in which we find ourselves will never be the temporal battle between health and disease but rather a spiritual war that will rage between faith and fear—trust and doubt.

- Is it possible to walk by faith through pain, suffering, and even death?

- Can one believe in the God who Heals even if healing isn't manifested now?

- Are you trusting for your healing or trusting the Healer?

These critical questions and many others will be addressed in the following pages. Be comforted. If you are sick and seeking God to heal you physically, don't give up on your healing. But more important, don't give up on the Healer. The most important weapon you have in your arsenal is not your faith, but the One in whom you trust. And while it may seem that the most important thing in life is being healed, you need to grow beyond that myth to the truth: the most important thing in life is Jesus because He alone is *life*!

The only time death and disease will defeat you is when your myths about healing replace the truth about the God who Heals. Now is the time to confront the myths, peel away the lies, and uncover God's truth to answer your most critical question: *When God doesn't heal now, is it still possible to walk by faith no matter what the circumstance?*

Confronting the myths and confessing the truth, you will discover for yourself that it is indeed possible to walk by faith no matter what happens!

Oh, that we could learn to believe the promises of God!
God has not gone back from His promises;
Jesus is still He who heals both soul and body;
    salvation offers us even now healing and holiness,
and the Holy Spirit is always ready to give us some
    manifestations of His power.
When we ask why this divine power is not more often
    seen, He answers us,
"Because of your unbelief."
Do not, then, let yourself be discouraged in your
    expectation,
even though God should delay to answer you,
or if your sickness be aggravated.
Once having placed your foot firmly on the
    immovable rock of God's own Word,
and having prayed the Lord to manifest His
    almightiness in your body
because you are one of the members of His body,
and the temple of the Holy Ghost,
persevere in believing in Him with firm assurance that
He has undertaken for you,
that He has made Himself responsible for your body,
and that His healing virtue will come to glorify Him
    in you.

—ANDREW MURRAY,
Divine Healing

CHAPTER 3

The Myth of Being Healed by Faith

John came to the altar for prayer during our morning worship service. It was a common and regular part of our worship to invite people who needed prayer to come forward at a particular point in worship. Scores would make their way to the altar as pastors, elders, and intercessors anointed with oil those who were sick and prayed in faith for their healing. Our practice of praying for the sick was rooted in the truths of Mark 16 and James 5.

> *Are any among you suffering? They should keep on praying about it. And those who have reason to be thankful should continually sing praises to the Lord. Are any among you sick? They should call for the elders of the church and have them pray over them, anointing them with oil in the name of the Lord. And their prayer offered in faith will heal the sick, and the Lord will make them well. And anyone who has committed sins will be forgiven. (James 5:13–15 NLT)*

They will lay hands on the sick, and they will recover.
(Mark 16:18)

So John came forward to the altar and kneeled at the prayer
rail. I stood behind the rail and knelt facing him as he extended
his hands to grasp mine. Tears streamed down his cheeks, and
his body trembled as he sobbed. Behind him stood his wife, one
hand resting on John's shoulder and the other raised heaven-
ward as she prayed in the Spirit silently and wept openly.

Intently John leaned forward and whispered, "I just got
back a lot of tests on Friday. The doctors say I have prostate
cancer. Pastor, I don't know if I have enough faith to go
through this. Will you pray for me?" As I anointed John with
oil and prayed with him for healing, my mind pondered the
phrase—*enough faith.*

For years I have heard preachers and teachers, evangelists
and laity imply that faith in some way is quantified. Such
myths seem to circulate unabated:

- If Susan had just had enough faith, she would have
  been healed.

- Bob's lack of faith caused him to miss his healing.

- When Bill's faith gets strong enough, he will be
  healed.

- If everyone in this room all believed at the same
  moment, then all would be healed.

- Because Joan lacked faith, she lost her healing.

And the myths go on like an endless freight train passing
through a busy intersection, stopping traffic for blocks. If we

could but unhitch the empty freight cars of myths and bring up additional engines of truth, our train of faith might really get somewhere instead of blocking the intersections of lives seeking earnestly to walk by faith.

Let me restate what I wrote earlier. When I call such statements "myths," I am not suggesting that they are devoid of truth. They may have been derived from actual experiences or even surmised from biblical texts. Myth is based on a limited experience not universal or absolute truth (see page xiv).

In fact, what makes these myths so appealing and even addictive in their use in various preaching and teaching circles is that they do have some basis in fact and some support in Scripture. But like an onion, when all the layers of experience and proclamation are peeled away, nothing of lasting substance remains at the core of a myth.

A myth serves us well for a time or a season or even an experience. Myths may contain true elements, but they cannot be substituted for absolute truth. A myth only seems true for some times, for some people, and in some situations.

If you are to understand why God doesn't heal now, you will have to peel away the layers of myth that have been so tantalizing for you to embrace. You will have to dig deep into Scripture for yourself instead of simply consuming the fast food of your favorite "pop" theologian. And you will have to decide to walk by faith instead of simply mouthing the platitudes of faith that have so easily supplanted God's Word in your daily confessions.

While the lack of faith may hinder healing, healing does not depend on faith. I have witnessed both the faithful and the faithless being healed. And I have seen those of great faith die. In fact, everyone that Jesus healed eventually died! Those around the tomb of Lazarus lacked faith, and certainly Lazarus was in no position to exercise faith—he had been dead four days (John 11:39). Yet, Lazarus experienced a wondrous healing; he was resurrected.

In Mark 2, a paralyzed man was lowered through a roof into a crowded room where Jesus was preaching. The faith of his friends apparently opened the roof and the way for his healing.

> Four men arrived carrying a paralyzed man on a mat. They couldn't get to Jesus through the crowd, so they dug through the clay roof above his head. Then they lowered the sick man on his mat, right down in front of Jesus. Seeing their faith, Jesus said to the paralyzed man, "My son, your sins are forgiven." But some of the teachers of religious law who were sitting there said to themselves, "What? This is blasphemy! Who but God can forgive sins!" Jesus knew what they were discussing among themselves, so he said to them, "Why do you think this is blasphemy? Is it easier to say to the paralyzed man, 'Your sins are forgiven' or 'Get up, pick up your mat, and walk'? I will prove that I, the Son of Man, have the authority on earth to forgive sins." Then Jesus turned to the paralyzed man and said, "Stand up, take your mat, and go on home, because you are healed!" (Mark 2:3–11 NLT)

When Jesus saw *their* faith not *his* faith, the man was both forgiven and healed. Faith may open up or begin the possibility for your physical healing or the healing of another person either *now* or *later,* but your healing or another's does not depend on your faith.

SEPARATING MYTH AND TRUTH

Earlier I likened a myth to an onion. You know something is there because there are taste and odor. However, if we peel away the layers of an onion, the center reveals that nothing remains. Myths are accumulated experiences and proof texts that when cooked together in the same pot result in a savory mix that tastes and smells good for the moment but lacks nourishment for the long, enduring walk of faith.

Faith is a marathon not a sprint. It doesn't matter how you start, only how you finish. You may start with strong, great faith only to end the race of life weak and faithless. Scripture encourages,

> Therefore, since we are surrounded by such a huge crowd of witnesses to the life of faith, let us strip off every weight that slows us down, especially the sin that so easily hinders our progress. And let us run with endurance the race that God has set before us. We do this by keeping our eyes on Jesus, on whom our faith depends from start to finish. He was willing to die a shameful death on the cross because of the joy he knew would be his afterward. Now he is seated in the place of highest honor beside God's throne in heaven. Think about all he endured when sinful people did such terrible things to him, so that you don't become weary and give up. After all, you have not yet given your lives in your struggle against sin. (Heb. 12:1–4 NLT)

Life's ultimate question that you face is not *Will you finish healed?* but rather, *Will you finish saved?*

Winning the race is not being healed. A man once said to

me after a friend's funeral, "Life's greatest enemy is death. She lacked faith. She doubted. So she lost and thus died." Yet this deceased friend was a believer who had surrendered her life to Jesus as Lord and Savior. She lives eternally with Christ in heaven. If death were the enemy, why would Paul write, "For to me, to live is Christ and to die is gain" or "We live by faith, not by sight. We are confident, I say, and would prefer to be away from the body and at home with the Lord" (Phil. 1:21; 2 Cor. 5:7–8 NIV)? We must avoid the myths of faith and healing and embrace the truths revealed in Scripture. Let's peel away the layers of three common myths about faith and healing.

MYTH #1: THE KEY TO MY HEALING IS MY FAITH

Some believers focus on faith as the key to healing. Yet Jesus healed many who apparently had no faith. Some were healed because their friends had faith. Others were healed even against their wills that were bound up by demonic spirits. In other words, they were healed through exorcism. The truth is that God heals. The myth is that God always heals *now* at the initiative of our faith.

Dr. Frederick K. C. Price asserted, "The seventh method of receiving healing—I believe is the highest kind of faith—is the highest way to receive healing . . . If you believe you receive it, you will confess that, 'Bless God—I believe I am healed. I believe I have received my healing.' . . . I believe that it is so. I believe that I can walk in divine health all the days of my life. You are reading after one man who will never be sick and I'm not being presumptuous."[1] Myth is mixed here with truth. The highest kind of faith is, "I believe in Jesus," not "I believe."

True, faith must be our initiative. But even our initiative comes through the prompting of the Holy Spirit: "No one can say that Jesus is Lord except by the Holy Spirit" (1 Cor. 12:3). Our faith helps us receive healing just as the lack of faith hinders healing, but healing does not depend on faith. Healing depends on the Healer.

Healing is the will of God. Peter Youngren wrote,

Jesus gave us two revolutionary concepts about healing. They contradict much of religious traditionalism, but they set you free and help you receive everything that God has for you. First, Jesus taught us that healing belongs to every believer . . .

The second powerful concept Jesus gave us is regarding His will. Jesus clearly shows us God's will in healing . . . Again the Word of God declares that "great multitudes followed Jesus and He healed them all" (Matt. 12:15).

When Jesus healed *all*, He was obviously doing the will of His Father, because He only did that which the Father wanted him to do. This is why you can come with boldness asking God for healing. God is on your side. He wants the best for you. He is good.[2]

So, if God wills all to be healed, then can your faith move His hand to heal you? In the words of the Hertz rental car commercial, *Not exactly!* Your faith moves Him to save you (Rom. 10:9–13; Eph. 2:8). And in your salvation is your healing: "This was to fulfill what was spoken through the prophet Isaiah: 'He took up our infirmities / and carried our diseases'" (Matt. 8:17 NIV; cf. Isa. 53:4–6). But your faith does not effect your healing *now*. *When* you are healed rests entirely on *what* the sovereign purposes of the Healer are.

Consider this biblical example. In John 5 Jesus healed one paralytic at the pool of Bethesda though a multitude thronged that place daily to be healed. Why was one man healed *now* while others were not? John 5:19 gives the answer when Jesus confessed, "I tell you the truth, the Son can do nothing by himself; he can do only what he sees his Father doing, because whatever the Father does the Son also does" (NIV).

Dr. Jack Deere correctly observed,

This verse gives one of the cardinal principles of Jesus' ministry: the initiative for the miraculous in Jesus' ministry did not begin with Him but with His Father. He healed only the people He saw His Father healing. The only firm reason for the healing of the paralytic that we can derive from the context of John 5 is that the Father willed it, and Jesus executed His Father's will. A similar explanation might be offered for the miraculous deliverance of Peter from prison in Acts 12. Why did the Lord allow James to be martyred, yet send an angel to deliver Peter from death? One might argue that it was because the church prayed for Peter, but without a doubt the church prayed for James also. We are ultimately faced with the conclusion that sometimes the Lord works miracles for His own sovereign purposes without giving any explanation for His actions to His followers.[3]

MYTH #2: IF I STAND FAST IN FAITH, I WILL BE PHYSICALLY HEALED IN TIME AND SPACE

Your healing will come—in time or in eternity. Ken and Gloria Copeland wrote, "If you have faith in your heart and God's Word in your mouth, healing will come. But it may take time for it to manifest in your body. So stand fast in faith, giving thanks to God until it does. Focus on God's Word, not on physical symptoms."[4] In what do we "stand fast"? The "rock" on which we stand isn't faith or healing but Christ—the Healer. In Hebrews 10:23 we are admonished to *hold fast to the profession of our faith*. But in what is our profession of faith? Certainly, it is not in faith or in healing.

Be careful to note that our faith is not *in faith*. Just believing hard enough, long enough, or strong enough will not strengthen you or effect your healing. Holding on to your miracle or your healing will not cause your healing to manifest *now*. I've heard people confess, "Well, if Sister Jones just holds on and keeps believing, she'll get her healing." The truth is that everyone who trusted Jesus in the first century A.D. died. In fact, many of the apostles died excruciating deaths and were even crucified. Did the apostles fail to hold on . . . did they lack faith . . . did they give up or quit? Certainly not. Did they miss their healing or fail to see healing manifested? Certainly not. In death, they were champions of faith:

Well, how much more do I need to say? It would take too long to recount the stories of the faith of Gideon, Barak, Samson, Jephthah, David, Samuel, and all the prophets. By faith these people overthrew kingdoms, ruled with justice, and received what God had promised them. They shut the mouths of lions, quenched the flames of fire, and escaped death by the edge of the sword. Their weakness was turned to strength. They became strong in battle and put whole armies to flight. Women received their loved ones back again from death. But others trusted God and were tortured, preferring to die rather than turn from God and be free. They placed their hope in the resurrection to a better life. Some were mocked, and their backs were cut open with whips. Others were chained in dungeons. Some died by stoning, and some were sawed in half; others were killed with the sword. Some went about in skins of sheep and goats, hungry and oppressed and mistreated. They were too good for this world. They wandered over deserts and mountains, hiding in caves and holes in the ground. All of these people we have mentioned received God's approval because of their faith, yet none of them received all that God had promised. For God had far better things in mind for us that would also benefit them, for they can't receive the prize at the end of the race until we finish the race. (Heb. 11:32–40 NLT)

So what is faith? It is more than believing in your heart that God heals. The truth is that God is the God who Heals. Faith is trusting the God who Heals. Faith is a radical, absolute surrender to the God who Heals. Faith is not holding on for your healing but holding on to the God who Heals.

The truth is that your healing may manifest in eternity, not in time. If your trust is in the God who Heals, then *when* He heals you is secondary to belonging to the Healer. Certainly you will thank Him if He heals you in time. But if your healing comes beyond death in eternity, will you praise Him now for that? Paul did just that: "'O Death, where is your sting? / O Hades, where is your victory?' The sting of death is sin, and the strength of sin is the law. But thanks be to God, who gives us the victory through our Lord Jesus Christ. Therefore, my beloved brethren, be steadfast, immovable, always abounding in the work of the Lord, knowing that your labor is not in vain in the Lord" (1 Cor. 15:55–58).

THE RELATIONSHIP BETWEEN FAITH AND HEALING

The Copelands urged us to stand fast in faith. Don't construct a myth around that encouragement. The myth is, *If you stand fast in faith, you will be physically healed in time and space.* The truth is, *If you stand fast in faith, trusting Jesus, you will be healed eternally even when you do not see your physicaly healing manifested* now.

Throughout the Gospels, faith plays an important role in some of Jesus' healing miracles. Jesus' ministry had three primary foci: proclaiming the kingdom of God, healing the sick, and delivering people from demonic bondages. Jesus often healed with a touch or a word. His simple method of healing seems centuries distant from many of the elaborate rituals and stylized formulas often witnessed in our healing services and crusades. We worship and praise God for hours, often seeing a crowd worked into an emotional frenzy as people sing, shout, and "fall under the anointing." In stark contrast, Jesus simply spoke a word, touched someone who was sick, or allowed Himself to be touched, and healing flowed from Him.

The relationship between faith and healing can first be seen by surveying Jesus' healing miracles. Here is a list of healing miracles from the Gospels and the method Jesus used to heal.

No. Healing	Matthew	Mark	Luke	John	Method
1. Man with unclean spirit		1:23	4:33		Exorcism, word
2. Peter's mother-in-law	8:14	1:30	4:38		Touch, word; prayer of friends
3. Multitudes	8:16	1:32	4:40		Touch, word; faith of friends
4. Many demons		1:39			Preaching, exorcism
5. A leper	8:2	1:40	5:12		Word, touch; leper's faith and Christ's compassion
6. Man sick of the palsy	9:2	2:3	5:17		Word; faith of friends
7. Man's withered hand	12:9	3:1	6:6		Word; obedient faith
8. Multitudes	12:15	3:10			Exorcism, response to faith
9. Gerasene demoniac	8:28	5:1	8:26		Word, exorcism
10. Jarius's daughter	9:18	5:22	8:41		Word, touch; faith of father
11. Woman with issue of blood	9:20	5:25	8:43		Touching His garment in faith
12. A few sick folk	13:58	6:5			Touch (hindered by unbelief)
13. Multitudes	14:34	6:5			Touch of His garment, friends' faith
14. Syrophoenician's daughter	15:22	7:24			Response to mother's prayer, faith
15. Deaf and dumb man		7:32			Word, touch; friends' prayer
16. Blind man (gradual healing)		8:22			Word, touch; friends' prayer
17. Child with evil spirit	17:14	9:14	9:38		Word, touch; friends' prayer
18. Blind Bartimaeus	20:30	10:46	18:35		Word, touch; compassion, faith

No. Healing	Matthew	Mark	Luke	John	Method
19. Centurion's servant	8:5		7:2		Response to master's prayer, faith
20. Two blind men	9:27				Word, touch; men's faith
21. Dumb demoniac	9:32				Exorcism
22. Blind and dumb demoniac	12:22		11:14		Exorcism
23. Multitudes	4:23			6:17	Teaching, preaching, healing
24. Multitudes	9:35				Teaching, preaching, healing
25. Multitudes	11:4		7:21		Proof to John the Baptist in prison
26. Multitudes	14:14		9:11	6:2	Compassion, response to need
27. Great multitudes	15:30				Faith of friends
28. Great multitudes	19:2				Various ways
29. Blind and lame in temple	21:14				Various ways
30. Widow's son			7:11		Word, compassion
31. Mary Magdalene and others			8:2		Exorcism
32. Woman bound by Satan			13:10		Word, touch
33. Man with dropsy			14:1		Touch
34. Ten lepers			17:11		Word; faith of the men
35. Malchus' ear			22:49		Touch
36. Multitudes			5:15		Various ways
37. Various persons			13:32		Exorcism, and not stated
38. Nobleman's son				4:46	Word; father's faith
39. Invalid man				5:1-15	Word; man's faith
40. Man born blind				9:1	Word, touch
41. Lazarus				11:1	Word

Faith plays an explicit part in sixteen of Jesus' healing miracles. In more than half of these healings, the faith does not rest in the one being healed but in another's faith for the sick person(s) to be healed. In twenty-five of the recorded healings, faith is not mentioned as a factor or method for healing.

In contrast to faith, Jesus' word appears to be a much more critical factor in *when* a person is healed. *When* Jesus speaks a word of healing, people are healed. In more than half of the recorded healings in the Gospels, Jesus either speaks a word, preaches, or teaches when healing occurs. Likewise, Jesus' touch or touching Jesus conveys healing in sixteen of the recorded healings.

When is healing *now*? The Gospels teach us some important truths:

- *When* Jesus speaks a word, healing is *now*.

- *When* Jesus touches or is touched, healing is *now*.

- *When* faith is expressed by others or the one being healed in the presence of Jesus, healing is *now*.

The quantity of faith is only mentioned in two healings. In Matthew 8:10 the centurion's "great" faith is mentioned as Jesus compared the centurion's faith (a Gentile) to the lack of faith by Israel. But Jesus did not heal the centurion's servant because of great faith. Rather, He simply pronounced healing "as you have believed" (Matt. 8:13).

In Matthew 15:28, the Syrophoenician woman's great faith is mentioned prior to the healing of her daughter. Jesus exclaimed, "O woman, great is your faith!" Great faith has less to do with quantity than with intensity. Faith is measured by degree more than by amount. Jesus spoke to this when He proclaimed in Revelation 3:15–16, "I know your works, that you are neither cold nor hot. I could wish you were cold or hot. So then, because you are lukewarm, and neither cold nor hot, I will vomit you out of My mouth." Jesus did not address amount but rather degree of intensity. He emphasized that even a minute faith could accomplish great things: "So Jesus said to them, 'Because of your unbelief; for assuredly, I say to you, if you have faith as a mustard seed, you will say to this mountain, "Move from here to there," and it will move; and nothing will be impossible for you'" (Matt. 17:20).

The lack of faith hinders healing. "And he [Jesus] did not do many miracles there [Nazareth] because of their lack of faith" (Matt. 13:58 NIV; cf. Matt. 21:32 NIV). In fact, the Greek word here (*apistos*) denotes unbelief or faithlessness. The absence of faith certainly restricts healing since the recipient, because of *apistos,* refuses to receive healing. But note that miracles still happen even in the midst of unbelief—*Jesus did not do many miracles* does imply that *some miracles* were done. Because Jesus is Lord, He can do what He wills regardless of our ability to believe or to receive.

Faith, healing, and Jesus. In all that has been said about faith or the lack of it, we have not yet mentioned the most important factor in Jesus' healing in the Gospels—*Jesus!* While faith, word, touch, obedience, and compassion all played significant parts in healing, only one factor was common to *all healings*—Jesus. In the Gospels and then later in Acts, the presence of Jesus is crucial to healing.

Filled with His Spirit and acting under the authority of His name, the apostles healed and delivered (cf. Acts 3:6; 4:10; 5:12ff.; 9:7ff.; 9:40ff.; 13:4ff.; 19:11ff.; 20:7ff.). The gifts of healing operate through the power of the Holy Spirit (1 Cor. 12:9), who is given to us by Jesus (John 15:26ff.; Acts 1:4ff.). When Jesus through the power of the Holy Spirit is present, healing happens according to His will. Jesus stated that His purpose as the Great Physician was to preach the gospel, heal the sick, and release captives: "The Spirit of the LORD is upon Me [Jesus], / Because He has annointed Me / To preach the gospel to the poor; / He has sent Me to heal the brokenhearted, / To proclaim liberty to the captives / And recovery of sight to the blind, / To set at liberty those who are oppressed; / To proclaim the acceptable year of the LORD" (Luke 4:18–19). So if Jesus is the crucial factor in healing, how does our faith truly function in healing?

MYTH #3: WHEN I CONFESS MY HEALING, I WILL BE HEALED NOW!

Confess the Healer, not your healing. As Frederick K. C. Price taught *Seven Scriptural Ways to Healing,* he identified Method 6 of healing as "Just Saying It." Dr. Price wrote:

This method—JUST SAYING IT with your mouth—not even praying about it—JUST SAYING IT WITH YOUR MOUTH—you shall have whatsoever you say—if you believe it in your heart—without doubting. YOU CAN SAY IT!

> *By just opening your mouth and saying, "Bless God, I*
> *believe that I receive my healing; I believe this tumor leaves*
> *now; I believe this cancer is cursed right now; I believe my*
> *needs are met right now; I believe this cataract has disinte-*
> *grated right now; I believe that my ears are open right now;*
> *I believe it is so."[5]*

What is the "it" that we say? We confess the "Jesus"—not the gift but the Giver.

In his best-selling book *The Bible Cure,* Dr. Reginald B. Cherry encouraged us to "speak to the mountain" of our illness when we pray.[6] That is important in prayer. But praying it and saying it don't make physical healing manifest *now.*

The myth constructed from such encouragements is, *When I confess my healing, I will be healed* now! Positive confession does not effect healing. Only Jesus heals. Our confession should be in Him, not in being healed *now.* Jesus sternly warned, "Therefore whoever confesses Me before men, him I will also confess before My Father who is in heaven. But whoever denies Me before men, him I will also deny before My Father who is in heaven" (Matt. 10:32–33).

The myths about faith and healing cloud the simple truth that God heals both now and in eternity. Here are the truths that counteract their corresponding myths:

MYTH	**TRUTH**
Believe and you will be healed now.	Faith does not heal. God heals.
Great faith heals.	The quantity of faith cannot effect healing.
God must heal when we believe.	The initiative of faith does not compel God to heal us.
God heals only those who believe.	God wills to heal all.
Whatever we confess by faith, God does.	When we confess Jesus, God saves.
The key to our healing is our faith.	The key to our healing is Jesus.
Persistent faith will cause healing to manifest.	Enduring faith finishes the race of life in victory.

I want to encourage you to trust Christ as your Healer. Claim Him as your Healer whether you see your healing manifest now or in eternity. Once you accept Jesus Christ as your personal Lord and Savior now, *when* you are healed becomes far less urgent in your walk of faith. Scripture never stresses that *now* is the time for your healing, but God's Word does declare, "I tell you, now is the time of God's favor, now is the day of salvation" (2 Cor. 6:2 NIV). Believing for your healing may actually become a hindrance to your believing Christ for your salvation. I have seen a number of people who, when they were not healed *now,* actually turned away from Christ in resentment and bitterness. Don't let that happen to you!

A. B. Simpson gave wise counsel on the role of faith and healing. Take his wisdom to heart:

Having become fully persuaded of the Word of God, the will of God and your own personal acceptance with God, now *commit your body to God and claim by simple faith His promise of healing in the name of Jesus.* Do not merely ask for it, but humbly and firmly claim healing as His covenant pledge, as your inheritance, as purchased redemption right. Claim it as something already fully offered you in the gospel and waiting only your acceptance to make good your possession.

There is a great difference between asking and taking, between expecting and accepting. You must take Christ as your Healer—not as an experiment, not as a future benefit, but as a present reality. You must believe that He does now, according to His promise, touch your life with His almighty hand and quicken the fountains of your being with your strength. Do not merely believe that He will do so, but claim and believe that He does now touch you and begins the work of healing in your body. And go forth counting it as done, acknowledging and praising Him for it.[7]

When God doesn't heal now, *trust Him to* begin *healing you now.* Even when physical healing manifests in time and space, that healing is merely temporal. Everyone whom Jesus healed finally died. All healing in time and space only begins the ultimate completion of healing in eternity. Healing our physical bodies is for His purpose and glory to accomplish His will. Healing us in body, soul, and spirit accomplishes the eternal salvation healing about which Paul jubilantly penned:

What I am saying, dear brothers and sisters, is that flesh and blood cannot inherit the Kingdom of God. These perishable bodies of ours are not able to live forever. But let me tell you a wonderful secret God has revealed to us. Not all of us will die, but we will all be transformed. It will happen in a moment, in the blinking of an eye, when the last trumpet is blown. For when the trumpet sounds, the Christians who have died will be raised with transformed bodies. And then we who are living will be transformed so that we will never die. For our perishable earthly bodies must be transformed into heavenly bodies that will never die. (1 Cor. 15:50–53 NLT)

TRUTHS ABOUT FAITH AND HEALING

When God doesn't heal *now*, you can apply essential truths about faith and healing that are anchored in Scripture. Like a muscle, faith must be exercised in order to grow in strength and effectiveness. James wrote, "Is any one of you sick? He should call the elders of the church to pray over him and anoint him with oil in the name of the Lord. And the prayer offered in faith will make the sick person well; the Lord will raise him up. If he has sinned, he will be forgiven. Therefore confess your sins to each other and pray for each other so that you may be healed. The prayer of a righteous man is powerful and effective" (James 5:14–16 NIV).

As you wait upon the Lord and pray for your healing, pray in faith. What is powerful and effective prayer *in faith*?

To walk in faith for healing both in time and for eternity, we must learn certain truths revealed in the healing miracles of Jesus. These key truths shatter shallow myths about faith and healing.

KEY TRUTH #1: HAVE OTHERS JOIN THEIR FAITH TO
YOURS IN BRINGING YOUR INFIRMITY TO JESUS

"When the sun was setting, the people brought to Jesus all who had various kinds of sickness, and laying his hands on each one, he healed them" (Luke 4:40 NIV; cf. Matt. 8:16; Mark 1:32; Mark 2:3ff.). When God doesn't heal now, don't try to go it alone. An essential key to healing in the New Testament is the power of corporate faith and praying in agreement with others (Matt. 18:19–20). When you gather with others to pray, the presence of Christ dwells in your midst. Since He is the Great Physician, with His presence comes healing power.

Throughout the healing miracle accounts in the Gospels, we observe that friends brought the sick to Jesus. In Mark 2:3ff., a paralytic man was brought by his friends to Jesus. The Syrophoenician woman brought her daughter to Jesus (Matt. 15:22; Mark 7:24). A father brought his demonized child to Jesus (Matt. 17:14; Mark 9:14; Luke 9:38).

Join your faith with others to seek the Great Physician. When sickness has weakened, fatigued, and discouraged you, seek out others who will pray in faith for you. *Don't go it alone!*

KEY TRUTH #2: BY FAITH, TOUCH JESUS

The woman with an issue of blood exercised her faith. She did all she knew to do and could do to reach out through a crowd and touch Jesus (Matt. 9:20ff.; Mark 5:24ff.; Luke 8:43ff.). When you are sick, the temptation will arise to isolate yourself from settings in which you can *touch and be touched* by the presence of Christ. At times, you may not feel like going to worship services; or you may feel too weak to sing and praise God; or you may be too tired and discouraged to call the elders to have them anoint you with oil and pray in faith for you. Resist the temptation to stay at home in isolation. Healing flows through the body of Christ; His body is the church.

Worship, sing, praise, pray, and gather with other believers to touch and be touched by Jesus.

KEY TRUTH #3: SUBMIT YOURSELF TO THE AUTHORITY
AND WILL OF CHRIST, TRUSTING HIM AS YOUR HEALER

The centurion's faith in Christ authoritatively opened a door for his servant to be healed. Likewise, the authority for your healing does not rest in you or your faith. Claiming your healing and speaking the right words do not guarantee your healing now or at any future time. Your faith opens a door for you to receive your healing from Christ.

I prayed with a woman who demanded that God heal her. When I asked her what she was doing, she exclaimed, "I have the authority as a child of God to command God to fulfill His promise of healing for me." She believed a myth. Our authority isn't over Christ but *in Christ*. We reign with Him in heavenly places (Eph. 2:4–7). The sons of Sceva presumed to have healing authority but quickly learned that authority rested in the person of Jesus, not simply in the recital of His name (Acts 19:13ff.).

The truth is that all authority for every matter including healing rests in Jesus: "All authority in heaven and on earth has been given to me" (Matt. 28:18 NIV). From Christ, we receive imparted authority (Mark 16:16ff.) to say what He says and to do what He does (cf. John 5:19). Submit to His authority for your healing.

KEY TRUTH #4: BELIEVE ON HIS WORD FOR
YOUR HEALING

Whenever Jesus spoke the word, people were healed (Matt. 8:8, 16; Luke 7:7). The psalmist declared that "he [the Lord] sent forth his word and healed them; / he rescued them from the grave" (Ps. 107:20 NIV). Listen to the word of the Lord for your healing. No one else's word, faith, or assurance will do. When God doesn't heal *now*, trust His voice and believe His Word.

Proverbs 4:20–22 reads, "My son, give attention to my words; / Incline your ear to my sayings. / Do not let them depart from your eyes; / Keep them in the midst of your heart; / For they are life to those who find them, / And health to all their flesh."

Kenneth E. Hagin wrote,

> In the margin of my *King James* translation, Proverbs 4:22 reads, "My words are *medicine* to all their flesh." God's Word is medicine to all your flesh, but you need to learn how to *take* God's medicine in order to get it to work for you. We know that faith comes by hearing, and hearing by the Word of God . . . (Rom. 10:17). But to tell you the real truth about the matter, God's Word, His medicine, won't do you a bit of good in the world if you heard it over and over again for hours yet still continued to think wrong and talk wrong.[8]

When God doesn't heal *now*, trust His Word, not your circumstances or human advice. Your healing doesn't depend on your faith, but on the One in whom you place your faith— Jesus, the Word![9]

O Saviour Christ, our woes dispel
for some are sick and some are sad;
And some have never loved you well,
and some have lost the love they had.
Your touch has still its ancient power
No word from you can fruitless fall;
Here in this joyful worship hour
And in your mercy, heal us all.

—HENRY TWELLS,
Prayers Across the Centuries

CHAPTER 4

THE MYTH OF BEING HEALED BY PRAYER

I don't know how to pray for my healing," Bill moaned. For years, Bill had prayed for the healing of others, but now when faced with the prospect of open-heart surgery he felt helpless. "I know all the right words and Scriptures, but they sound so empty and powerless to me now," he confessed.

Positive confession implies that the way we pray and the words we use can unlock the mysteries of healing. At times, the myths associated with prayer and healing seem to be more akin to magical incantations and mystical spells than to what James calls powerful and effective prayer (James 5:16). Here are some of the myths circulating about healing prayer:

- Right prayer produces right results.

- Praying and applying the blood heals the sick.

- When we pray and confess those things that are not as though they are, prayer brings spiritual healing into the visible realm.

- When two agree regarding anything in prayer, God must act; He must heal.

Remember, a myth may combine experience and Scriptures that seem to work for a time, while a truth can be applied for all people, at all times, and in all situations. Let's examine some particular situations in which people prayed for healing, but God did not heal *now*.

WHEN WE PRAY AND GOD DOESN'T HEAL *NOW*

Earlier I shared the story of William and Alicia. They prayed continually for Alicia's healing from liver cancer. Elders prayed and anointed Alicia with oil. Friends and intercessors around the country prayed. Yet their story reveals that when God didn't heal *now*, they still prayed.

William partly believed a myth about prayer. He confided, "You are trying to make God do what you want when you pray. Did I want my wife healed? You bet I did. I loved her. And there is nothing more in the world that I wanted than to have her healed. I knew God had a plan. And I wanted His plan fulfilled in our lives. We prayed for God to reveal to us any medical steps He wanted us to take. We exhausted every pathway we knew in the spiritual and the natural to see if His answer was there for us."

One myth about prayer and healing that William clung to for months was simply this: *When you pray rightly, God must act and heal now—in time and space.* However, prayer cannot manipulate God. Some preachers proclaim, "Your prayers will move the hand of God." The purpose of prayer is to effect the Father's will in heaven on earth (Matt. 6:10). We do not pray to move God to our place, but rather for Him to move us to His place of healing.

Some teach that we should never pray, "Lord, if it be Thy will, heal so-and-so." Such a prayer mixes doubt into the dough of faith, resulting in the bread of confusion. God doesn't need an "out" just in case He chooses not to heal *now*. Praying for healing does not need to focus on convincing God to heal. He is the God who Heals. Prayer never informs God of His nature or questions His character. The truth is that healing is for everyone:

- "That evening many demon-possessed people were brought to Jesus. *All* the spirits fled when he commanded them to leave; and he healed *all* the sick. This fulfilled the word of the Lord through Isaiah, who said, 'He took our sicknesses and removed our diseases'" (Matt. 8:16–17 NLT, emphasis added).

- "Then Jesus went about all the cities and villages, teaching in their synagogues, preaching the gospel of the kingdom, and healing *every* sickness and *every* disease among the people" (Matt. 9:35, emphasis added).

- "And when He had called His twelve disciples to Him, He gave them power over unclean spirits, to cast them out, and to heal *all* kinds of sickness and *all* kinds of disease" (Matt. 10:1, emphasis added).

- "And wherever he went—into villages, towns or countryside—they placed the sick in the marketplaces. They begged him to let them touch even the edge of his cloak, and *all* who touched him were healed" (Mark 6:56 NIV, emphasis added; cf. Matt. 14:36).

Healing is for *all*. Praying for healing is in the will of God. A. B. Simpson wrote,

> A mere vague trust in the possible acceptance of your prayer is not faith definite enough to grapple with the forces of disease and death. The prayer for healing, "if it be Thy will," carries with it no claim for which Satan will quit his hold. This is a matter about which you ought to know His will before you ask, and then you must will and claim it because it is His will.
> Has God given you any means by which you may know His will? Most assuredly. If the Lord Jesus has purchased healing for you in His redemption, it must be God's will for you to have it, for Christ's whole redeeming work was simply the executing of the Father's will. If Jesus has promised it to you, it must be His will that you should receive it, for how can you know His will but by His Word?[1]

I visited the hospital room of an older church member who had prayed in faith for healing for many years. She was scheduled for the surgical removal of kidney stones and had been suffering from excruciating pain for days. The X rays had revealed some stones the size of golf balls, so the doctors had diagnosed that passing the stones would be impossible.

As I entered her room, she excitedly greeted me, "Pastor, come pray with me and agree with me for my complete healing. I am not going to surgery this morning. By His stripes, I am healed."

Somewhat taken by surprise, I limply held her hand and piously began a beautiful, stained-glass intonation, "Dear God, if it be Thy will, heal Mrs. Thomas from her affliction . . ."

Interrupting me with measured impatience, she instructed, "God has already healed me. That's His will for me. And my affliction is kidney stones. Pray for God to shatter those stones and keep me away from the surgeon's knife this morning."

I attempted to pray as she instructed while she loudly "Amened" and praised the Lord throughout my prayer. Upon looking up, I came face-to-face with her anesthesiologist.

"Mrs. Thomas," the doctor soothingly said, "you will be in surgery soon to remove your kidney stones. Do you have any questions?"

"I certainly do," she replied. "Will you order a new set of X rays? I am healed from my kidney stones. My pastor here prayed with me, and God has healed me."

We were in a Baptist hospital, and I assumed that healing prayer would not be so great an anomaly for him. But his shocked and perplexed look betrayed him. Shaking his head, her doctor sternly warned, "Mrs. Thomas, we cannot do that. The gurney is right outside your door, and they are ready to transport you to surgery. We cannot schedule X rays."

"I will not go to surgery. If you will not take a new set of X rays, I will lie right here until my family doctor arrives and insist that he does what I ask," she stubbornly replied.

Still shaking his head in disbelief, the anesthesiologist left the room. "Pastor, wait right there," she instructed. So I took a seat near her bed and began to talk with her. A few minutes later, Mrs. Thomas's family doctor did arrive in her room making rounds. After he listened to her story and request for X rays, her family doctor acquiesced to her request.

Soon a portable X-ray machine arrived in the room. I left her to visit other patients from my congregation and promised to return later. After a few hours, I revisited a smiling, laughing Mrs. Thomas who happily reported, "Well, Preacher, you are some kind of prayer warrior. The X rays showed no sign of stones, and I am checking out at noon."

I did the obligatory "Praise God's" and hurriedly left the room to retreat back to my mainline church's pastor's study and review my notes about prayer and healing. Mrs. Thomas was the first person I ever prayed with who was healed *now*!

So, did my prayer heal Mrs. Thomas? Of course not! God healed Mrs. Thomas. But I wonder if we might have missed God's timing for a miracle had we not prayed. Maxie Dunnam, in teaching on intercessory prayer, once posed the question, "What if there are some things God either cannot or will not do until people pray?" That question leads us into disarming the myths and asserting the truths about prayer and healing.

WHEN GOD DOESN'T HEAL *NOW,* PRAY!

In Scripture, prayer is never presented as an option; rather, it's a command. Here is a sampling of texts on prayer (emphasis added):

- "'For I know the plans I have for you,' declares the LORD, 'plans to prosper you and not to harm you, plans to give you hope and a future. Then you will call upon me and come and *pray* to me, and I will listen to you. You will seek me and find me when you seek me with all your heart'" (Jer. 29:11–13 NIV).

- "But I tell you: Love your enemies and *pray* for those who persecute you" (Matt. 5:44 NIV).

- "This, then, is how you should *pray*: 'Our Father in heaven, / hallowed be your name'" (Matt. 6:9 NIV).

- "In the same way, the Spirit helps us in our weakness. We do not know what we ought to *pray* for, but the Spirit himself *intercedes* for us with groans that words cannot express" (Rom. 8:26 NIV).

- "*Pray* continually" (1 Thess. 5:17 NIV).

- "And *pray* in the Spirit on all occasions with all kinds of *prayers* and requests. With this in mind, be alert and always keep on *praying* for all the saints" (Eph. 6:18 NIV).

- "Do not be anxious about anything, but in everything, by *prayer* and petition, with thanksgiving, present your requests to God" (Phil. 4:6 NIV).

- "Is any one of you sick? He should call the elders of the church to *pray* over him and anoint him with oil in the name of the Lord" (James 5:14 NIV).

Prayer opens the door for us to receive healing, but it doesn't force the healing to come through the door. And inept prayer doesn't lock the door. Frederick K. C. Price remarked,

YOU MUST AGREE. The method here is AGREEING. IF YOU ARE NOT AGREEING, IT [PRAYER] WON'T WORK.

That is the reason that many Christians you have prayed for have died.

You wonder—"Why did they die? We were praying for them to be healed."

What you didn't know was that all the time the person was hoping to go on to Glory. You wanted them healed, but he was ready to die. There is no agreement there, and God can't answer that prayer . . .

Sometimes when I pray for people and I tell them, "Look, we will agree, and I will lay hands on you, and we are going to believe that you receive your healing, according to the Word of God. Is that all right with you?"

"Yes, Yes," they say.

"Will you believe that God heals you now?" I ask.

"Yes, yes."

I lay my hands on them in all confidence and faith and I pray—and I sometimes feel the power of God flowing into their bodies. I know that God has sent His healing power into them.

When I get finished with the prayer, I say, "Well, bless God, do you believe you are healed?"

"I certainly hope so," they reply.

Well—see we didn't agree. I am believing that they are healed, and they are hoping so. Can you see? That is not agreement. That won't work.[2]

MYTHS THAT HINDER EFFECTIVE, POWERFUL PRAYER

Our desire and passion for prayer can be hindered and quenched when shallow myths invade our minds as we pray for healing. These three myths hinder prayer:

MYTH #1: PRAYER COMPELS GOD TO HEAL

There are some possible myths that we might deduce from the teaching about praying in agreement quoted above by Dr. Price. While the encouragement to believe and agree in prayer is important, agreeing in prayer does not force God's hand to heal *now*. And while not praying may certainly hinder our ability to receive healing, healing does not depend on prayer. Let's take one simple example from Scripture: "God did extraordinary miracles through Paul, so that even handkerchiefs and aprons that had touched him were taken to the sick, and their illnesses were cured and the evil spirits left them" (Acts 19:11–12 NIV). There is no indication that Paul prayed over the handkerchiefs and aprons to impart God's healing power nor is there a report that those receiving these specially anointed objects were praying for healing. Nonetheless, they were healed.

Healing depends upon the Healer. Our prayers provide the venue for God to act and to heal us and others. But prayer neither compels God to heal *now* nor does it limit His healing power.

MYTH #2: SIMPLE PRAYER IS INEFFECTIVE PRAYER THAT LIMITS GOD'S HEALING POWER

Does praying "in Jesus' name" or "by His stripes" or "through the blood of Jesus" make a prayer effective? Is there a formula or a certain set of Scriptures that must be prayed in order for God to heal? When Jesus healed, both His healing words and prayers were surprisingly simple.

Arriving into the pentecostal-charismatic movement from a mainline denomination was quite a theological jolt for me. But many kind people were ready and eager to teach me how to pray for the sick. Anointing with oil was usually required. Praying over a person in the Spirit or in tongues was often necessary. Commanding spirits of infirmity, disease, and specifically speaking to those spirits—spirits of cancer, diabetes, heart disease, etc.—was also part of my instruction in proper, effective praying for healing. Quoting numerous verses was also recommended, particularly the healing passages from Exodus 15, Psalms 103 and 107, Isaiah 53, Matthew 8, and 1 Peter 2.

While I am still doing all of the above as God's Spirit leads, I have realized upon a careful reading of Jesus' healing ministry—and He is the ultimate type for healing—that praying for the sick can be just as effective and powerful when it is short and sweet!

Praying effectively and with power is rooted in righteousness (James 5:16) not in ritual.

Jesus healed with a few words such as "Be clean!" (Mark 1:41 NIV) or "Be opened!" (Mark 7:34 NIV). Once He took mud and spit into it to make a healing ointment and commanded a blind man to go wash in a pool for his healing (John 9). And when He prayed for Lazarus's healing, He prayed simply, "Father, I thank you that you have heard me. I knew that you always hear me, but I said this for the benefit of the people standing here, that they may believe that you sent me" (John 11:41 NIV). Then Jesus simply commanded, "Lazarus, come out!" (John 11:43 NIV). With that simple prayer and word, Jesus raised the dead.

MYTH #3: IF THE RIGHT PERSON PRAYS FOR ME, I WILL BE HEALED

How often I have heard people tell of rushing to a healing evangelist's crusade or a special healing service to have the "man" or "woman" of God pray for them. No one else would do. Yet, 1 Corinthians 12 asserts that gifts of healing have been freely given by the Holy Spirit to the body of Christ. Those gifts can flow through a nobody as easily as through a somebody. *Jesus* heals the sick, not Roberts, or Hinn, or Hagin, or Price. The truth is simply this: Healing flows through a vessel and, when God chooses, He doesn't even need the vessel!

The disciples were worried about the right people healing the sick in Jesus' day.

> "Teacher," said John, "we saw a man driving out demons in your name and we told him to stop, because he was not one of us."
>
> "Do not stop him," Jesus said. "No one who does a miracle in my name can in the next moment say anything bad about me, for whoever is not against us is for us. I tell you the truth, anyone who gives you a cup of water in my name because you belong to Christ will certainly not lose his reward." (Mark 9:38–41 NIV)

In Belgrade, a young university student came to me after a worship service and asked me if I would go home with her and pray for her atheistic father who was ill. She believed that if I would go and pray, something special would happen. And should her father be healed *now*, then he might accept Christ.

"Why don't *you* go home and pray for him to be healed?" I asked.

"He would never let me. But he would let you because you are an American preacher. You are an important dignitary in our country," she protested.

"Go home and pray for your father's healing," I instructed. "Ask him if you might pray for him to get well. I truly believe he will allow it."

Before the next evening's service, this student excitedly rushed up to me and hugged me. "I prayed for my father last night. He let me pray for him, and he told me this morning that he feels well. He is healed. He asked me all about Jesus." Her prayers were powerful and effective because they were the right thing to do at the right time. She prayed humbly and in submission to her father's permission. The right person to pray for healing is the person God has anointed and chosen for that moment to pray.

POWERFUL AND EFFECTIVE PRAYER FOR HEALING

What is the most effective and important thing you can do when God doesn't heal *now*? How is one to pray effectively and powerfully for healing? Though prayer doesn't heal, prayer does open us up to receive healing as we hear God's voice and are led by His Spirit. Consider Hezekiah.

Hezekiah, king of Judah, was one who prayed. When Sennacherib, king of Assyria, threatened Jerusalem with the mightiest army of the day, Hezekiah went to the temple and prayed (2 Kings 19:14ff.). He took Sennacherib's threatening letter to the temple and spread it out before the Lord. Hezekiah prayed specifically about his problem.

When God pronounced through the prophet Isaiah that Hezekiah would not recover from his illness and would die, Hezekiah prayed.

In those days Hezekiah became ill and was at the point of death. The prophet Isaiah son of Amoz went to him and said, "This is what the LORD says: Put your house in order, because you are going to die; you will not recover." Hezekiah turned his face to the wall and prayed to the LORD, "Remember, O LORD, how I have walked before you faithfully and with wholehearted devotion and have done what is good in your eyes." And Hezekiah wept bitterly. Before Isaiah had left the middle court, the word of the LORD came to him: "Go back and tell Hezekiah, the leader of my people, 'This is what the LORD, the God of your father David, says: *I have heard your prayer and seen your tears; I will heal you.* On the third day from now you will go up to the temple of the LORD. *I will add fifteen years to your life. And I will deliver you and this city from the hand of the king of Assyria. I will defend this city for my sake and for the sake of my servant David.*'" (2 Kings 20:1–6 NIV, emphasis added)

Praying for your healing makes a difference. So when God has not healed *now,* how, then, should you pray? Apply these truths about prayer when seeking God for healing:

Pray humbly. Hezekiah prayed out of a broken and contrite heart. He had been obedient and humble before God. Though he was king, he did not have an arrogant, proud attitude. David wrote, "You do not delight in sacrifice, or I would bring it; / you do not take pleasure in burnt offerings. / The sacrifices of God are a broken spirit; / a broken and contrite heart, / O God, you will not despise" (Ps. 51:16–17 NIV).

Pray boldly, persistently in faith. When he had a need,

Hezekiah boldly approached God. He immediately came before God with his cry. In the New Testament, a remarkable example of boldly approaching the Lord can be found in Matthew 15:21–28. A Canaanite woman approached Jesus, begging Him to heal her daughter. Her cry was bold, direct, and intense: "Lord, Son of David, have mercy on me! My daughter is suffering terribly from demon-possession" (Matt. 15:22 NIV). For a Gentile woman to approach a Jewish rabbi took courage, boldness, faith, and persistence. She specifically asked for her need and persevered even when Jesus rebuffed her appeal.

> Jesus did not answer a word. So his disciples came to him and urged him, "Send her away, for she keeps crying out after us." He answered, "I was sent only to the lost sheep of Israel." The woman came and knelt before him. "Lord, help me!" she said. He replied, "It is not right to take the children's bread and toss it to their dogs." "Yes, Lord," she said, "but even the dogs eat the crumbs that fall from their masters' table." Then Jesus answered, "Woman, you have great faith! Your request is granted." And her daughter was healed from that very hour. (Matt. 15:23–28 NIV)

Both Hezekiah and the Canaanite woman refused to let delay stop their prayers. Hezekiah's reign was interrupted by an illness and a word from God that he would die. If anything might convince a sick person that God would not heal now or ever it would be a direct, prophetic word: *You will die!* That didn't stop Hezekiah from praying.

Another impediment to prayer might be *no answer*. Have you been praying but receiving no answer? If you have, then don't stop praying. Refuse to quit. Hezekiah could have stopped when the word of the Lord came. The Canaanite could have given up when Jesus gave no answer. In spite of illness, delay, or rebuke, continue to press on with prayer.

Pray continually (1 Thess. 5:17). When God doesn't heal *now*, the temptations are to complain; become discouraged, resentful, or bitter; quit; give up; turn to human answers, advice, and solutions; or to stop praying altogether. If prayer opens the door to receiving your healing, then prayerlessness shuts the door, and bitter resentment locks it!

Pray in faith for your need. Jesus commended the faith of the Canaanite woman. Her faith had intensity, boldness, passion, and urgency. She took the initiative to seek out Jesus.

> The Canaanite woman has a desperate need and deep faith in Jesus. She is in no mood to hear reasons why the two may not be joined together in a joyful healing. She refuses to accept second-class citizenship in the religious caste system of the day as a reason why her daughter must live a stunted life. She overcomes Jesus' reluctance by focusing on the gifts he has to offer and on the deep need her people have for them. She does not waste time or energy taking offense. She persists, and in desperation her faith sparks boldness and ingenuity in her.[3]

Pray for others. Both Hezekiah and the Canaanite woman were intercessors. Before Hezekiah had prayed for himself, he had prayed for his people to be delivered from the enemy. The Canaanite woman was not asking for herself but for her daughter and indirectly for her people—Gentiles.

James wrote, "Pray for one another" (5:16), and Paul urged, "Keep on praying for all the saints" (Eph. 6:18 NIV). When Job prayed for his friends, "the LORD made him prosperous again and gave him twice as much as he had before" (Job 42:10 NIV).

Pray with praise. When you focus on all God has done for you through His Son, and you stop focusing on your illness, then you will uncover the secret to praying for your healing— praise! Eternal healing and salvation have been sealed in the redeeming death of Christ (Isa. 53). Praise Him for that. Join the psalmist:

> Praise the LORD, O my soul;
>> all my inmost being, praise his holy name.
> Praise the LORD, O my soul,
>> and forget not all his benefits—
> who forgives all your sins
>> and heals all your diseases,
> who redeems your life from the pit
>> and crowns you with love and compassion,
> who satisfies your desires with good things
>> so that your youth is renewed like the eagle's.
>
> (Ps. 103:1–5 NIV)

Pray in His name and will. When we pray in the name of Jesus, we are praying under His authority, by His power, and in His will. In praying in His will, we are always seeking God's purpose, in His timing, done in His way for His glory. Jesus promised, "I tell you the truth, anyone who has faith in me will do what I have been doing. He will do even greater things than these, because I am going to the Father. And I will do whatever you ask in my name, so that the Son may bring glory to the Father. You may ask me for anything in my name, and I will do it" (John 14:12–14 NIV).

Father of the Reformation, Martin Luther, denied the gifts of healing in his era. However, the year before he died—1545—Luther was asked what to do for a man who was mentally ill. Luther wrote instructions for a healing service based on James 5 and said, "This is what we do, and that we have been accustomed to do, for a cabinetmaker here was similarly afflicted with madness and we cured him by prayer in Christ's name."[4]

Pray to receive. Believe it or not, some people enjoy being sick! They like the attention and see themselves as victims instead of victors. They seek pity. Their illness provides them with an excuse to abort God's purpose and potential in their lives. James admonished us not to take it lying down when we are sick. Instead, we are to call the elders for prayer (James 5:14). Like Hezekiah and the Canaanite woman, we must take the initiative and be ready to receive all God has for us.

When Jesus approached the invalid lying beside the pool of Bethesda, He asked, "Do you want to get well?" (John 5:6 NIV). In other words, are you ready to receive?

Pray with another in agreement. Corporate prayer with the saints and praying with another prayer partner are powerful. Jesus taught, "Again I say to you that if two of you agree on earth concerning anything that they ask, it will be done for them by My Father in heaven" (Matt. 18:19). For years I have prayed with my wife when either one of us has been attacked by illness. Yes, we seek medical attention when it is necessary. Dr. Cherry wrote that God has a *pathway to healing* each of us that may involve both natural and super-natural healing. We have found that to be true. And we have discovered that as we pray for healing, God reveals to us by His Word and Spirit the pathway we are to take.

Don't wait until a major illness strikes to pray. Pray in agreement for God to heal when headaches, colds, and body aches arise. If you cannot trust God to heal minor illnesses, how will you ever pray in agreement for major diseases? Becky Tirabassi wrote, "Praying with others for God's intervention in any given situation creates excitement and incentive to keep agreeing in prayer! Lost wallets, potential job opportunities, hopeful marriage partners, finances, the mending of relationships, from details to dreams—agreeing prayer is a faith-building experience, not to be neglected or considered as powerless."[5]

Pray the Word. The Word is God's powerful scalpel to incise all sin and sickness from our lives (cf. Heb. 4:12f.). The Word is a mighty sword repelling any attack against us spawned by the enemy (Eph. 6:10–18). Jesus used the Word of God in the wilderness to repel every temptation and attack of Satan (Matt. 4). God sends forth His Word for healing (Ps. 107:20).

> Prayer and the Word are inseparably linked together. Power in the use of either depends upon the presence of the other. The Word gives me guidance for prayer, telling me what God will do for me. It shows me the path of prayer, telling me how God would have me come. It gives me the power for prayer, the courage to accept the assurance that I will be heard. And it brings me the answer to prayer, as it teaches what God will do for me. And so, prayer prepares the heart

for receiving the Word from God Himself, for the teaching of the Spirit which gives spiritual understanding, and for the faith that carries out God's will.[6]

The truth is that prayer opens us to receive God's healing while prayerlessness closes us to God's ministering Spirit. While powerful, effective prayer opens us to healing, God's healing doesn't depend on prayer but on the One to whom we pray—Jesus. Keep praying, fixing your focus not on your illness but on Him.

The source of all illness is Satan. Jesus tells us very clearly that the devil has come to steal, kill and destroy (John 10:10).

Jesus came to give us abundant life. God is the giver of good gifts—not evil gifts (James 1:12–17).

Our own destructions open the door to sickness and sin in our lives.

Our own failures to take care of our bodies can lead to disease and illness.

We need to ask God to use the Holy Spirit to reveal the destructions that we are bringing upon our own bodies.

He will show us things that we are doing wrong.

He will reveal any addictions or sin habits that open the door to Satan.

When we understand that Jesus is the Healer, we will turn to His Word for revelation about all healing.

—REGINALD B. CHERRY, M.D.,
The Doctor and the Word

CHAPTER 5

THE MYTH OF DISEASE BEING GOD'S PUNISHMENT

Patty sat in my church office for her first counseling session. She was an attractive mother in our congregation who had raised three beautiful children, had an adoring husband, and by all appearances was joyfully walking by faith in her Christian journey. Yet, her demeanor on this day was somber and on the verge of weeping.

"I have a confession," she admitted, and as she did so tears began to stream down her cheeks. My mind raced through its mental checklist of potential crises that might have precipitated her reaction: adultery, gossip, prayerlessness, or marital conflict. None seemed to register with what I knew about Patty after having been her pastor for more than three years.

"I have a lump in my breast and a pap smear that is precancerous. I am so scared and so sorry . . ." Her sobs interrupted her confession, and she wept for the next few minutes.

I asked our bookkeeper to come into the office, and together we prayed for Patty's healing and rebuked any spirit of fear in her life. As we prayed, she continued to weep and say over and over again, "Lord, I am so sorry."

After we prayed she regained her composure and continued, "I know why I have cancer in my breast and reproductive organs. I sinned sexually before I married Chad, and now God is punishing me. What I sowed, I am now reaping. I never told Chad that years before we married, when I was in high school, I sinned sexually and became pregnant. I couldn't tell anyone, especially my parents. My boyfriend paid for my abortion, and no one ever knew but him, me, and God. O God, I am so sorry . . ." With that pent-up confession held in for decades, Patty descended into a pool of tears and self-condemnation.

She believed a myth—*God punishes us with disease because of sin.* This myth dresses itself in a number of dark, condemning garments:

- *Unconfessed sin "finds us out" through manifesting itself in sickness and disease.*

- *God punishes those who sin with a disease attacking us physically that will expose the sin.*

- *The sins of and curses upon preceding generations will infect us with disease.*

- *Whatever we sow in sin, we will reap in disease.*

It is true that the law of sowing and reaping does play a part in health. We cannot constantly eat foods laced with harmful fats and expect our bodies not to be affected. The

Torah warned, "This shall be a perpetual statute throughout your generations in all your dwellings: you shall eat neither fat nor blood" (Lev. 3:17). Such fatty foods have been demonstrated to increase substantially the risk of heart disease and cancer.[1]

It is also true that when we sow negative things into our lives, what we sow can be destructive to our souls and bodies. Sowing hate or anxiety can give rise to psychosomatic diseases. Constant stress can produce health problems such as ulcers, colon diseases, heart problems, etc. We also know that sins of addictions and abuse are often passed on from generation to generation (Ex. 20:5). So the law of sowing and reaping is a natural law arising out of our fallen state of sin. Paul wrote about this in Galatians: "Do not be deceived: God cannot be mocked. A man reaps what he sows. The one who sows to please his sinful nature, from that nature will reap destruction; the one who sows to please the Spirit, from the Spirit will reap eternal life. Let us not become weary in doing good, for at the proper time we will reap a harvest if we do not give up" (6:7–9 NIV).

Having said all that, the crux of the issue concerning this myth is not original sin or the law of sowing and reaping. The myths focus on quite another question: *Does God inflict us with disease to punish us for sin?* Patty was tormented by the condemning thought that her cancer came upon her as the result of God's punishment for her sexual immorality and having an abortion years earlier. As we talked together, Patty revealed that she had repented of her past sins and received the forgiveness of the Lord years ago. But the appearance of cancer in her life brought her under fresh feelings of condemnation for past sin. It is possible that unconfessed, unrepented sin could become a death-inflicting blow in our lives as in the lives of Ananias and Sapphira (Acts 5). But is repentance sufficient to cleanse us from sin—body, soul, and spirit? Could Patty be correct in feeling that her disease was punishment wrought by a vengeful, angry God?

Certainly, Patty's loving Father, the God who Heals, did not and would not send cancer to punish her. Two examples from Scripture quickly dispel this myth. John wrote, "But if we walk in the light as He is in the light, we have fellowship with one another, and *the blood of Jesus Christ His Son cleanses us from all sin.* If we say that we have no sin, we deceive ourselves, and the truth is not in us. *If we confess our sins, He is faithful and just to forgive us our sins and to cleanse us from all unrighteousness*" (1 John 1:7–9, emphasis mine).

Similarly, Jesus addressed this issue when He healed the blind man in John 9:2–3: "'Teacher,' his disciples asked him, 'why was this man born blind? Was it a result of his own sins or those of his parents?' 'It was not because of his sins or his parents' sins,' Jesus answered. 'He was born blind so the power of God could be seen in him'" (NLT).

The healing power of Christ overcomes myths about past sin and also human traditions that seek to condemn us when we have sickness in our lives. Knowing the human predisposition to regard disease as a punishment for sin, Jesus forgave the paralytic man before He healed him in Mark 2:1–12. Job's friend tried to convince him that his suffering and illness were inflicted by God as punishment for sin in his life (Job 4:7ff.). Yet, God rebuked the friends of Job who tried to condemn him (Job 42:7ff.).

SIN CONFESSED IS NOT REMEMBERED!

You may be fighting a terrible disease at this very moment and wondering why God doesn't heal you now. Believing the myth that God is using your disease to punish you, you may be experiencing tremendous guilt and condemnation. How difficult it is to receive God's healing while still under condemnation! Paul wrote, "There is therefore now no condemnation to those who are in Christ Jesus, . . . for the law of the Spirit of life in Christ Jesus has made me free from the law of sin and death" (Rom. 8:1–2).

Years ago I heard a story by Keith Miller. It seems that a few years back the charismatic movement was sweeping through various Catholic parishes in remote areas of the Southwest. Because of their small sizes and remote locations and with the shortage of priests, many of them were without priests, and a few had nuns who oversaw much of the spiritual life in these parishes.

In one of the tiny parishes, revival broke out. At the center of the revival whirlwind was a nun who was reported to be God's instrument for the performing of many signs and wonders. Scores were saved, healed, and delivered through her ministry. So the bishop of that diocese wanted to investigate further the reports and the character of this nun.

The bishop ordered her to travel many miles to the large city in which the bishop resided. Calling her into his office, the bishop inquired of this pious nun, "Sister, I understand that revival has come to your parish and that the Lord often does signs and wonders through you."

"Yes," she quietly replied.

"And does the Lord tell you to do these things?" he asked.

"Yes, He does," she answered.

"Then you hear the Lord's voice, and you speak with the Lord directly?"

"Yes, that is true," confided the nun.

"I must verify this for myself," the bishop continued. "When you return to your parish and speak to the Lord, ask Him what the bishop's secret sin is that he confessed only to the Lord and no other. Then come back and tell me what the Lord says. Only He knows my confessed sin. And if you report back accurately about what my sin was, then I will know you are speaking with the Lord and that what you are doing can be confirmed as truly from God."

"Yes, Bishop," she agreed and returned to her parish.

Weeks followed by months passed, and the bishop had no report from the nun. However, the reports of increasing signs and wonders did reach his office, so he knew that this remarkable nun must be hearing from the Lord. Finally, the bishop's patience came to an end. He called the nun and demanded that she travel immediately to his office with her report.

When the nun entered the bishop's office, the bishop impatiently asked her, "Sister, have you been talking with the Lord?"

"Yes," she meekly replied.

"And did you ask the Lord what I instructed you to ask?" the bishop abruptly asked.

"Yes," she answered.

"So . . . what did the Lord tell you was the bishop's secret confessed sin?" he asked.

"The Lord said He didn't remember," replied the nun.

If you are feeling condemnation for past, confessed sin, this story is for you. Your illness may be an attack of the enemy or the result of your abusing your body, but it is not punishment from the Lord. Here is God's promise to you: "'And they will not need to teach their neighbors, nor will they need to teach their family, saying, "You should know the LORD." For everyone, from the least to the greatest, will already know me,' says the LORD. *'And I will forgive their wickedness and will never again remember their sins'*" (Jer. 31:34 NLT, emphasis added).

WHY AM I SUFFERING?

You may be asking yourself, "So if my suffering is not punishment from God, then why am I suffering?" This question may be piercing your heart right now. Trials and tribulations are purposed by God to produce hope in our lives. As Paul wrote, "We can rejoice, too, when we run into problems and trials, for we know that they are good for us—they help us learn to endure. And endurance develops strength of character in us, and character strengthens our confident expectation of salvation. And this expectation will not disappoint us. For we know how dearly God loves us, because he has given us the Holy Spirit to fill our hearts with his love" (Rom. 5:3–5 NLT; cf. 1 Peter 1:3–9). However, instead of growing stronger in your faith and hope through trials and suffering, you may simply find yourself asking more questions and growing more skeptical as pain wears away any veneer of hope you may have struggled to maintain.

Earlier in the book, I shared with you the story of Alicia, who died of cancer. As William and Alicia faced what seemed like endless days of pain, they asked this very question. Their daughter confided, "I searched for reasons why

Mom was suffering so. Others around us suggested that maybe there was a curse on the family. Maybe Mom didn't believe hard enough. Maybe there were some Scriptures she should have been quoting and listening to that she wasn't. We were teachable and willing to receive any biblical instruction we needed to face Mom's cancer. I reached out for help. Some days, almost hourly, Mom would be vomiting and praying at the same time, 'Jesus, please help me. Here, here I am. I praise You, Lord. Jesus, even if You don't heal me the way I want, I love You and praise You and believe that everything will be okay.' At times, Mom would stop right in the middle of doing something and shout, 'No, devil, I will not accept that.' She was focused on Jesus and refused to be tempted by the devil or any human being to focus on anything other than that which was good, pure, and holy."

Alicia fought to maintain hope in the face of increasing pain and weakness. As she grew physically weaker, Alicia asked many questions of me, her family, and her Lord. Some of the answers she received gave her comfort, but many other questions remained unanswered.

You may come to believe some of the answers you receive as to why you are suffering. But none of these answers will completely answer all the questions you have for the Lord, nor will they satisfy every need you have. The apostle Paul himself suffered from a thorn in his flesh that tormented him. He prayed to the Lord three times to have the thorn removed, and God did not heal him. So Paul came to this revelation:

> I have plenty to boast about and would be no fool in doing it, because I would be telling the truth. But I won't do it. I

don't want anyone to think more highly of me than what they can actually see in my life and my message, even though I have received wonderful revelations from God. But to keep me from getting puffed up, I was given a thorn in my flesh, a messenger from Satan to torment me and keep me from getting proud. Three different times I begged the Lord to take it away. Each time he said, "My gracious favor is all you need. My power works best in your weakness." So now I am glad to boast about my weaknesses, so that the power of Christ may work through me. Since I know it is all for Christ's good, I am quite content with my weaknesses and with insults, hardships, persecutions, and calamities. For when I am weak, then I am strong. (2 Cor. 12:6–10 NLT)

The *myth* is, *God is punishing you with disease.*
The *truth* is, *Confessed sin is forever cleansed by the blood of Christ in which there is salvation, forgiveness, healing, and deliverance.*

It is also true that you may never receive all the answers you need to answer all the questions you have. And out of the boggy mysteries of unanswered whys may arise mud that you will use to make bricks—bricks of doubt and discontent. And from these bricks you may choose to construct walls between you and the God who Heals that may keep you from receiving either His comfort or His healing—or both.

If you allow the myth that your disease is God's punishment to persist in your life, then you will build walls between you and the Lord. These walls can isolate you from the purposes of God for your life.

THE WALLS THAT HINDER YOUR RELATIONSHIP WITH THE GOD WHO HEALS

When God doesn't heal now, you may be tempted to construct walls between yourself and the Healer. Those walls are built with the bricks of disappointment, discouragement, resentment, and bitterness. Believing the myth that God uses disease to punish you will add the straw to your bricks, making the walls you build between you and God formidable. Let's identify these walls so you can tear down existing ones and avoid building new ones.

THE WALL OF UNKEPT PROMISES

You will be tempted to believe that God has not kept His healing promises in your life. In fact, you may witness others being healed and hear their exciting testimonies only to feel that God's promises were true for them but not for you. This is the enemy's way to discourage you and fill you with doubt and disbelief.

The truth is that God has already fulfilled all of His promises in Christ Jesus. You may not have yet witnessed in time and space the manifestation of your healing, but that in no way nullifies the truth that in Christ you are saved, healed, and delivered. Paul wrote,

> But as surely as God is faithful, our message to you is not "Yes" and "No." For the Son of God, Jesus Christ, who was preached among you by me and Silas and Timothy, was not "Yes" and "No," but in him it has always been "Yes." For no matter how many promises God has made, they are "Yes" in Christ. And so through him the "Amen"

is spoken by us to the glory of God. Now it is God who makes both us and you stand firm in Christ. He anointed us, set his seal of ownership on us, and put his Spirit in our hearts as a deposit, guaranteeing what is to come. (2 Cor. 1:18–22 NIV)

You have a guarantee that you will be healed—the Holy Spirit. The Spirit will help you pull down any wall of unkept promises you may have built between you and God. Ask the Spirit to help you pray (Rom. 8:26ff.): "Almighty God, pull down this wall in my relationship with You. I claim Your eternal promise to save, heal, and deliver me. In Jesus' name, amen."

THE WALL OF UNMET NEEDS

If you are tempted to believe that God is not meeting your needs, then you will build a wall of unmet needs that becomes a self-fulfilling prophecy. Your needs will not be met because your wall separates you from the very One who can meet them.

Your primary need in life is Christ. Denying that He meets your needs cuts you off from His healing power and compassionate mercy. Paul wrote, "And my God will meet all your needs according to his glorious riches in Christ Jesus" (Phil. 4:19 NIV). Jesus warned us not to focus on tomorrow or worry about what may happen. Your anxiety about unmet needs tomorrow will hinder you from receiving all that you need from Christ today. So Jesus instructed, "But seek first his kingdom and his righteousness, and all these things will be given to you as well. Therefore do not worry about tomorrow, for tomorrow will worry about itself. Each day has enough trouble of its own" (Matt. 6:33–34 NIV).

In keeping this wall torn down, consider praying continually the prayer that St. Patrick offered up to the Lord:

> *I call upon Christ to protect me today,*
> *Against poison, against burning, against drowning,*
> *　　against death-wound.*
> *Until a multitude of rewards come to me!*
> *Christ with me, Christ before me, Christ behind me,*
> *　　Christ in me!*
> *Christ below me, Christ above me, Christ at my right,*
> *　　Christ at my left!*
> *Christ in breadth, Christ in length, Christ in height!*
> *Christ in the heart of everyone who thinks of me,*
> *Christ in the mouth of everyone who speaks to me,*
> *Christ in every eye that sees me,*
> *Christ in every ear that hears me!*
> *I awake today to a strong virtue, an invocation of the*
> *　　Trinity.*
> *I believe in a threeness with confession of a oneness, in*
> *　　the Creator of the universe.*
> *Salvation is the Lord's, salvation is the Lord's, salvation*
> *　　is Christ's.*
> *May Thy salvation, O Lord, be always with us.*[2] *Amen.*

With Christ as your all in all, no wall of unmet need can ever be constructed between you and God your Healer.

THE WALL OF UNFULFILLED EXPECTATIONS

You may have expected God to have healed you when . . .

- you called the elders and they came, anointing you with oil and praying for you.

- a healing evangelist gave a word on television that someone with your condition was being healed right now.

- a pastor, evangelist, or minister prayed for your healing at the altar.

- you prayed and claimed the promises of God for yourself.

- friends laid hands on you and prayed for your healing.

- someone gave you a personal word from the Lord or prophesied over you that you were healed.

Receiving and believing for your healing in that moment, you rejoiced and expected to see your physical healing manifested—if not instantly, at least over a period of time as you experienced a divine healing process. However, nothing was manifested, and as days and weeks passed, the beacon of your hope dimmed, and your expectations shattered on the rocks of the reality that your condition was worsening instead of improving.

As expectation gave way to despair, you may have started constructing a wall of unfulfilled expectations. Your prayers may have become a recital of all that God didn't do instead of all that He promised. So what now is left for you? Your wall has blocked all light of hope and cast dark shadows over your future.

When the truth is known, walls of unfulfilled expectations are whitewashed sepulchres threatening to bury not only our hopes but our very lives. How do you keep the wall of unfulfilled expectations torn down? Never expect a person, a service, a program, or a prescribed ritual to heal you. Anchor your hope in nothing less than Jesus' blood and righteousness.

Firmly build your foundation for healing on the Healer. Hold fast to the truth that it "is Christ in you, the hope of glory" (Col. 1:27).

THE WALL OF UNCONFESSED SIN

Your desire to hold on to past guilt and sin can block the healing power of the Healer. A. B. Simpson warned,

> *Be careful that you are right with God.* If your sickness has come to you on account of any sinful cause, be sure that you thoroughly repent of and confess your sins and make all restitution as far as it is in your power. If sickness has been a discipline designed to separate you from some evil, at once present yourself to God in frank self-judgment and consecration and claim from Him the grace to sanctify you and keep you holy. An impure heart is a constant fountain of disease.[3]

Your unconfessed sin can become such an onus to God that you will be stricken now instead of healed now as evidenced in Acts 5 with Ananias and Sapphira. If a wall of unconfessed sin separates you from the Healer, hear the God who Heals call out to you,

> Why should you be beaten anymore?
>   Why do you persist in rebellion?
> Your whole head is injured,
>   your whole heart afflicted.
> From the sole of your foot to the top of your head
>   there is no soundness—
> only wounds and welts
>   and open sores,

not cleansed or bandaged
    or soothed with oil . . .
"Come now, let us reason together,"
    says the LORD.
"Though your sins are like scarlet,
    they shall be as white as snow;
though they are red as crimson,
    they shall be like wool." (Isa. 1:5–6, 18 NIV)

THE WALL OF UNRESOLVED ANGER

Perhaps the most persistent temptation of all that you will face in illness is to become angry and bitter with God. James wrote about this:

What is causing the quarrels and fights among you? Isn't it the whole army of evil desires at war within you? You want what you don't have, so you scheme and kill to get it. You are jealous for what others have, and you can't possess it, so you fight and quarrel to take it away from them. And yet the reason you don't have what you want is that you don't ask God for it. And even when you do ask, you don't get it because your whole motive is wrong—you want only what will give you pleasure. (4:1–3 NLT)

Are you angry with God for not healing you *now*? Do you become angrier when God heals others and not you, especially when the others healed may be less holy or faithful than you feel yourself to be? Does your ire rise up when another is healed the first time they pray, when you have been praying for healing for months or even years? Are you praying with a pure motive, or has bitterness taken root in you? "See to it that no one misses the grace of God and that no bitter root grows up to cause trouble and defile many" (Heb. 12:15 NIV). Angry bitterness will become a wall that cuts you off from the healing grace of God.

If the wall of unresolved anger has infected your soul and separated you from the God who Heals, then repent of your anger and return to God. Pray Psalm 51 as your prayer to tear down the wall of unresolved anger.

THE WALL OF UNFORGIVENESS

This final wall that you may be tempted to build is capable of not only hindering your healing, it can also threaten your salvation. Jesus clearly warned, "For if you forgive men when they sin against you, your heavenly Father will also forgive you. But if you do not forgive men their sins, your Father will not forgive your sins" (Matt. 6:14–15 NIV). There may be someone between you and your healing. You may have been deeply offended by another person. As John Brevere warned, offenses are the bait of Satan. This bait, once taken, traps the one offended in a miry bog of ongoing recriminations and blame.

If there is someone in your life whom you cannot forgive, that offense cuts you off from the ability to even worship God. Jesus taught, "Therefore if you bring your gift to the altar, and there remember that your brother has something against you, leave your gift there before the altar, and go your way. First be reconciled to your brother, and then come and offer your gift" (Matt. 5:23–24). Paul warned that we should not be guilty of sinning against the body and blood of Jesus. When we partake of the Lord's Supper we are to examine ourselves and not take of it in an unworthy manner (1 Cor. 11:27ff.).

Billy Joe Daughtery told this story about unforgiveness:

We have a friend who has been teaching and preaching for over 60 years. Both she and her husband have ministered the fullness of the Word of God faithfully and have walked in His unfailing love and provision.

In 1964, having walked in divine health for many years, our friend was attacked by cancer. She underwent the recommended surgery, and while recuperating sought the Lord as to how or why this thing had come upon her.

God revealed to her that she had allowed unforgiveness to spring up in a root of bitterness in her heart. She had been ill treated by a sister in the church years before, and had not released the hurt and anger that followed. When her spirit bore witness to this, she knew exactly how she had allowed the devil entrance into her body. She immediately promised the Lord that as soon as she got out of the hospital she would go to that sister and resolve the difference. She did so. She totally recovered and she has not had any recurrence of cancer or any serious problem in the last 26 years!

To discern the Lord's body is to examine yourself to make sure there is nothing blocking your faith . . . that there is no blockage to receiving the healing Jesus bought at Calvary . . . understanding what Jesus did at Calvary.[4]

Tear down the wall of unforgiveness. Go to the person with whom you are offended. Forgive them and ask their forgiveness. In doing so, you will tear down the wall between you and that person as well as between you and God. Then you will be able to receive the forgiving and healing grace of the God who Heals.

TEAR DOWN THE WALLS

Tearing down one of the aforementioned walls will not be easy. We become comfortable with our walls, believing the lie that walls will protect us.

Actually, just the opposite is true. Walls keep us from seeing the truth and receiving all that God wants to do in and through us.

You can begin the process now of tearing down the walls. Here are some simple first steps:

- *Repent.* Take your wall to God. Confess and repent that it is there, and then turn away from your wall, never to return again.

- *Release.* Release all the negative feelings and attitudes you have had and all the negative words you have spoken about what God hasn't done for you.

- *Renew.* Renew your faith and love of the Lord. Focus on the God who Heals instead of on your sickness.

- *Replace petition with praise.* God knows your need. Instead of praying vainly the same petition for healing over and over again, begin to praise God for all He has done, is doing, and will do in your life.

Tearing down walls between you and God will be a continual process. You will be tempted almost daily to build a new wall. Don't give in to the negative process of making bricks out of sin and building a wall of separation between you and your Healer. Each time you feel tempted to move away, do the opposite of what you feel and move near to God.

Experience this promise:

So humble yourselves under the mighty power of God, and in his good time he will honor you. Give all your worries and cares to God, for he cares about what happens to you. Be careful! Watch out for attacks from the Devil, your great enemy. He prowls around like a roaring lion, looking for some victim to devour. Take a firm stand against him, and be strong in your faith. Remember that Christians all over the world are going through the same kind of suffering you are. In his kindness God called you to his eternal glory by means of Jesus Christ. After you have suffered a little while, he will restore, support, and strengthen you, and he will place you on a firm foundation. All power is his forever and ever. Amen. (1 Peter 5:6–11 NLT)

IS YOUR DISEASE A WALL?

The myth is: *God is punishing you with disease.*
The truth is: *You may be allowing your disease to come between you and God.*
While God does not punish you with disease, your disease may have built a wall between you and the God who loves you. Don't let your disease become a wall between you and God.
Set everything aside, including your desire to be healed. Seek Him alone. Desire His presence more than anything He can give or do for you. Tear down every wall between you and your Healer.

Some trust in chariots and some in horses,
but we trust in the name of the LORD *our God.*
They are brought to their knees and fall,
but we rise up and stand firm.

—KING DAVID,
Psalm 20:7–8 NIV

CHAPTER 6

THE MYTH OF BEING TOUCHED BY THE RIGHT PERSON

When I helped in the healing lines at various crusades and healing services, three types of people would rush forward with the hope of being on the platform to be touched by the evangelist, faith healer, pastor, or speaker. First came the person who had been healed in the service through a word of knowledge given by the speaker. Second came the person who had not been healed but who desperately wanted to be touched and prayed for by the speaker. Finally those came who did not need healing but simply wanted the speaker to pray for a problem or situation in their lives. At times, they even desired to "stand in" for a family member or friend who needed healing. They believed that the speaker could pray for them and then they would take that speaker's healing anointing back to the person who needed a healing touch.

At one evening healing service my wife and I attended, I earnestly desired to experience the healing anointing of God's Spirit. I prayed for the Spirit to show me people being healed as the speaker spoke words of knowledge about those in the service being healed. I wanted different people who were being healed to be shown to me by the Spirit. I felt that if the Holy Spirit were truly healing people, then He could certainly reveal them to me as well as to the healing evangelist on the platform. Then during the testimony time, those people could announce their healing, and I would know for certain that the Spirit was present and healing people that evening.

As I prayed, I saw in my mind's eye a screen of various organs and limbs being healed. Though my eyes were shut as I prayed and saw these visionary scenes of healing, I wrote on a piece of paper all that I saw by the Spirit. My wife sat next to me, surprised and wondering what I was doing. Like a videotape of healing, I saw in the Spirit a liver and kidney healed. A neck calcified over from some form of injury was healed with all the calcium deposits melting away. Injuries and diseased organs were being healed right before my mind's eye. The last healing I envisioned was a man's fractured right ankle being completely made whole. Scribbling my last note, I excitedly whispered to my wife what I had seen. She shook her head in disbelief as I reviewed the list of eleven healings I had spiritually seen.

The evangelist invited those who had been healed to come down to the platform and give their testimonies. Perhaps a hundred or more rushed forward. One by one they marched across the platform and shared their healing testimonies. At times, they reiterated the healing word spoken by the evangelist from which they claimed and experienced healing. But to my excitement, a number of people specifically mentioned healing after healing that the Spirit had shown me. By the end of the testimony time, I had checked off ten of the eleven healings. Ecstasy filled me like electric charges. I had seen for myself God's healing power revealed apart from a famous healing evangelist. The Spirit could and would reveal His healing power to anyone who sought Him.

Yet one detail disturbed me. The man with a broken ankle had not given a testimony. I was ready to believe that he had been healed and simply not come forward to testify when a loud, shrill yell boomed forth from the back of the auditorium. A man on crutches with an ankle cast rushed forward toward the platform, wildly swinging the crutches over his head.

"I'm healed! I'm healed!" he shouted as he ran up onto the platform. "My ankle was broken. That's why I have the cast. But I felt heat all through my ankle. I can put my full weight on it." He ran across the front completely healed. I checked off the last item on my list.

The myth is: *In order to be healed, the right person must touch us.*

The truth is: *In order to be healed, the Holy Spirit must touch us.*

The person who lays hands on us is only a vessel; he or she is not the instrument of healing. Too often I have heard people exclaim that if only Benny Hinn or Oral Roberts or so-and-so prayed for them or touched them then they would be healed. Namaan believed such a myth, and he was proved wrong!

HEALED THE WRONG WAY?

From Naaman's perspective, God's pathway to his healing was wrong when the "right" person refused to meet him, much less touch him or pray for his healing. Naaman was a Syrian general who learned from his servant girl that a Jewish prophet, Elisha, could cure him of his leprosy.

Now both Naaman and his handmaiden believed a myth: *that a man could heal.* The girl said to Naaman's wife, "If only my master were with the prophet who is in Samaria! For he [the prophet Elisha] would heal him of his leprosy" (2 Kings 5:3). Even Naaman's king bought the myth and sent Naaman with money and a letter to Elisha so that "you [Elisha] may heal him of his leprosy" (2 Kings 5:6).

Elisha recognized the myth and completely demythologized the general's thinking by refusing to see him. Instead, Elisha sent a messenger to the door when Naaman arrived looking for the man of God to touch and heal him. "Go and wash in the Jordan seven times, and your flesh shall be restored to you, and you shall be clean" (2 Kings 5:10).

Was Naaman elated at the prospect of his healing? Not exactly! Instead of rejoicing, Naaman threw a temper tantrum and refused at first to bathe in the Jordan. He wanted healing his way, not God's. He had sought a man to touch and heal him, not a river. The truth is that God can use any instrument He chooses through which to convey His healing touch. Throughout the Bible, God used staffs, laying on of hands, water, mud, breath, a river, spit, anointing with oil, handkerchiefs, shadows, words, and people through which to impart His healing.

To believe that healing rests in a person is like believing surgery can be successfully done with a scalpel. God uses but doesn't need people for healing. Remember Hezekiah? God instantly healed him while the king lay on his sickbed praying.

Throughout the book of Acts, at the hands of the apostles many signs and wonders were done and people were healed (5:12; 14:3; 19:11; 28:8). Mark 16:18 commands believers to lay hands on the sick and they will be healed. But having the "right" person lay hands on you will not heal you. Healing comes through God's direction for the "laying on of hands."

Your healing will never depend on anyone's touch but the Master's. All He touches and who touch Him are healed. Too many evangelists and Christian personalities are elevated to celebrity status by Christian "fans" simply because God uses them as instruments of healing. The one ministering the gifts of healing is not the healer. The Spirit gives the gifts and thus imparts God's healing power.

When God doesn't heal now sometimes occurs when our eyes and faith are fixed on people, not on Jesus. From whom are you seeking your healing?

WHEN GOD'S POWER GETS DISTORTED

Avoiding the myth of believing that people heal requires us to make a deliberate choice to fix our eyes on the Giver not the gift, on God's power not God's man or woman. In Acts 8 a sorcerer named Simon desired the power of the Holy Spirit: "When Simon saw that the Spirit was given at the laying on of the apostles' hands, he offered them money and said, 'Give me also this ability so that everyone on whom I lay my hands may receive the Holy Spirit'" (vv. 18–19 NIV).

Peter strongly rebuked Simon and told him that his heart was not right before God. Simon repented. You may need to repent. You may be looking for someone to heal you. You may be going from person to person, evangelist to evangelist, meeting to meeting, hoping to be touched by the Spirit's power through a person. You may be placing your hands on TV sets hoping to get healed when a televangelist prays for viewers. You may be buying holy oil from Israel. You may even be trying to buy your healing as Simon did by sending offerings to various healing ministries. Your efforts will not get you healed!

TURN FROM MYTHS TO THE TRUTH

In this and the past three chapters we have examined the myths we are tempted to believe about healing. Faith, prayer, and the right people cannot heal us. Disease is not God's punishment, and sin cannot keep us from being healed. Jesus has come to save, heal, and deliver us from sin, disease, and death.

My dear friend Sam Hinn has preached and written, "We are never changed in the presence of a man. We are only changed in the presence of God." That truth is so applicable to healing.

The myth is: *We are healed in the presence of a man.*

The truth is: *We are only healed in God's presence.*

When God doesn't heal now, and we have believed the Truth—Jesus—and not myths, what must we then understand in order to walk by faith through pain, suffering, and even facing death?

Understand that *when* God heals has much to do with God's timing and sovereignty as God declared in Exodus 15:26, "I will put none of the diseases on you which I have brought on the Egyptians. For I am the LORD who heals you."

Andrew Murray encouraged us:

Let us learn to see in the risen Jesus the divine Healer, and let us receive Him as such. In order that I may recognize in Jesus my justification, my strength, and my wisdom, I must grasp by faith that He is really all this to me; and equally when the Bible tells me that Jesus is the sovereign Healer, I must myself appropriate this truth, and say, "Yes, Lord, it is Thou who art my Healer."[1]

Are you ready to discover how to walk by faith in the God who Heals? If so, let's uncover in the next chapters important truths about:

- God's timing
- God's sovereignty
- Walking by faith through valleys
- Claiming God's promises
- Celebrating victory over disease and death

Don't resent God for seeming failure to keep His word,
But trust and praise Him for His tender concern for you
and His perfect timing.

—HAROLD BREDESEN,
Need a Miracle?

CHAPTER 7

GOD'S TIMING

When God Doesn't Heal Now focuses on the issue of timing not reasoning. We cannot schedule this "right time" for healing based on our opinions or rationale. Rarely does God's timing "make sense" to us. Reasoning can never solve the mystery of *whys:*

- Why doesn't God heal now?
- Why am I sick?
- Why do I suffer?
- Why are others healed and I am not?

Nor can reasoning solve the mystery of *when:*

- When will I be physically healed?
- When will God answer?
- When will God act?

Reasoning may follow divine revelation, but it can never precede it. I can ponder, meditate, and reflect on what God has revealed, but I cannot reason out what He should reveal. Reasoning can never contain divine revelation since reasoning is finite and divine revelation is infinite.

If you have trusted human reason or wisdom to help you understand why you are sick or when you will be healed, you may have found yourself to be frustrated or even angry with God. Paul had already anticipated the shortcomings of human reason and wisdom.

> Where is the wise? Where is the scribe? Where is the disputer of this age? Has not God made foolish the wisdom of this world? For since, in the wisdom of God, the world through wisdom did not know God, it pleased God through the foolishness of the message preached to save those who believe. For the Jews request a sign, and Greeks seek after wisdom; but we preach Christ crucified, to the Jews a stumbling block and to the Greeks foolishness, but to those who are called, both Jews and Greeks, Christ the power of God and the wisdom of God. Because the foolishness of God is wiser than men, and the weakness of God is stronger than men. (1 Cor. 1:20–25)

At the crux of *when God doesn't heal* is timing not reasoning. If God would reveal *when* He heals, then all of our *whys* would dissolve as the early morning mist under the heat of a noonday sun.

If we try to reason *when* God will heal, then we will be forced to create myths to answer. Reasoning about *when God heals* forces the creation of myths such as

- God will heal *when* my faith is great enough.

- God will heal *when* my prayers or the prayers of others are righteous, powerful, and effective.

- God will heal *when* He is finished punishing me.

- God will heal *when* the right person touches me.

When put to the test of time, myths always fail us. They wreck on the rocks of doubt and despair as the winds of pain and suffering finally shipwreck our faith in everything or everyone but the true object of faith—the God who Heals.

Setting aside all myths, what does God reveal in His Word about *when*? Does God heal in eternity? Does God heal in time and space? What has He revealed about *when* He heals?

"I AM THE GOD WHO HEALS YOU"

God has revealed that healing is in His nature and character. The eternal I AM revealed in Exodus 15:26, "If you diligently heed the voice of the LORD your God and do what is right in His sight, give ear to His commandments and keep all His statutes, I will put none of the diseases on you which I have brought on the Egyptians. For I am the LORD who heals you."

Throughout the Old Testament, God revealed His name in different places to describe His nature. God is **Creator** (Gen. 1), **Almighty** (Gen. 17:1), **Provider** (22:14), **Sanctifier** (Ex. 31:13), and **Healer** (Ex. 15:26), just to list a few of His names.

God acted in time and space to heal throughout Scripture. God performed mighty healing miracles through Elijah (1 Kings 17) and Elisha (2 Kings 4–5). We have already listed the healing miracles in the Gospels and overviewed some of the healings in Acts. And God also acted in history beyond the first century A.D. to heal.

I am indebted to Eddie Hyatt who researched and collected a number of historical sources, far too numerous to quote entirely here, that confirm the healing power of the Holy Spirit through history. I have previously studied all of the writings that he researched in patristics and church history. Here is a brief survey of a few of the healing references made in these historical writings.[1]

HEALING IN CHURCH HISTORY

The early church fathers reported numerous healings. The Bishop of Lyons, Iranaeus (A.D. 125–200), reported, "Others still heal the sick by laying their hands upon them, and they are made whole. Yea, moreover, as I have said, the dead even have been raised up, and remained among us for many years. And what shall I more say? It is not possible to name the number of gifts which the Church [scattered] throughout the whole world, has received from God in the name of Jesus Christ."[2]

Another prominent leader of the early church, Origen in Alexandria, Egypt, reported that marvelous cures were done through God's power with many people "freed from grievous calamities, and from distractions of mind, and madness, and countless other ills."[3] Bishop Athanasius in writing *The Life of Antony* (A.D. 252–356) described the father of monasticism, Anthony, as one "through [whom] the Lord healed the bodily ailments of many present, and cleansed others from evil spirits."[4] Other church fathers through whom miraculous healings occurred were Pachomius (A.D. 292–346), Hilarion (A.D. 305–385), and Benedict of Nursia (ca. A.D. 480–547).

Augustine (A.D. 354–430), the bishop of Hippo in North Africa, became fascinated with God's healing power late in his life. He wrote, "Miracles were wrought in the name of Christ," and then proceeded to report various healings from a multitude of diseases.[5] And as the church moved into the Middle Ages, Gregory the Great (A.D. 540–604) recorded many healing miracles that he had personally witnessed.[6]

The writings about the life of Dominic (A.D. 1170–1221) and St. Francis of Assisi (A.D. 1181–1226) abound with stories of healing miracles surrounding their lives. In the last half of the twelfth century, a renewal movement was birthed within the Roman Catholic Church by Peter Waldo (A.D. 1217). The descendants and followers, called Waldenses, witnessed many healing miracles and confessed their belief in healing: "Therefore concerning the anointing of the sick, we hold it as an article of faith, and profess sincerely from the heart that sick persons, when they ask it, may lawfully be anointed with anointing oil by one who joins them in praying . . . such an anointing performed according to the apostolic design and practice will be healing and profitable."[7]

One of the leading reformers, Martin Luther (1483–1546), said, "Often has it happened, and still does, that devils have been driven out in the name of Christ; also by calling on His name and prayer, the sick have been healed."[8]

Founder of the Quakers, George Fox (1624–91), wrote

his famous journal reporting healing miracles, *Journal* and *Book of Miracles*. Count Zinzendorf (1700–1760) organized the Moravians and wrote of healing miracles: "We have had undeniable proofs thereof in the unequivocal discovery of things, persons and circumstances which could not humanly have been discovered, in the healing of maladies in themselves incurable, such as cancers, consumptions, when the patient was in the agonies of death, all by means of prayer, or of a single word."[9]

John Wesley, founder of Methodism, wrote of how God miraculously healed him at various times throughout his ministry: "I do not recollect any Scripture wherein we are taught that miracles were to be confined within the limits of the apostolic age or the Cyprian age, or of any period of time, longer or shorter, even till the restitution of all things."[10]

In recent years I have done extensive research in the writings of Azusa Street (and William Seymour), John G. Lake, Maria Woodworth-Etter, Kathryn Kuhlman, Smith Wigglesworth, and others in the twentieth-century healing movements. The summary of all this must simply be the undeniable truth: *God is the God who Heals, both in Scripture and throughout history, from the early church to the present-day church.*

Later in this book, we will explore the healing promises of God in Scripture. The reason God promises to heal is simple: God's nature is to save, heal, and deliver. Of course, the Greek name Jesus, from the Hebrew *Yeshua* or Joshua, literally means "God saves." And the verb from which the name Jesus is derived is *sozo*, which means both "to save" and "to heal" (Acts 4:9; 14:9; James 5:15).[11]

The triune God is the God who heals. God the Father

heals; God the Son is the Great Physician; and God the Spirit imparts the gifts of healing.

HEALING IN TIME AND ETERNITY

Picture a ruler. Let that ruler represent time. History is a linear progression of time with a beginning and an end. Now picture that ruler completely submerged in a tank of water. The water completely surrounds the ruler in every way.

The ruler represents time with a fixed beginning (alpha) and a fixed end (omega). Jesus is the Alpha and the Omega, the beginning and the end (Rev. 1:7). The Great Physician stands at the beginning and end of history. God is the Eternal One (Deut. 33:27). The triune God surrounds and encompasses history as that water encompasses the ruler.

The good news for us is that God has already been where we are going. He knows what's in front of us; He's forgiven what's behind us; and He's with us right *now*.

God has been where you are going—there's nothing to fear. God has been where you've been—there's nothing to hold on to, all is forgiven. God is where you are—there's no way He'll leave you alone.

God has completed in eternity all that is started in history. He knows the end from the beginning. God never starts anything that He hasn't already finished. So Revelation boldly declares, "All who dwell on the earth will worship him, whose names have not been written in the Book of Life of the Lamb slain from the foundation of the world" (Rev. 13:8). In the blood of the Lamb, God eternally saved, healed, and delivered those who trusted in Jesus

Christ as Lord and Savior. That eternal, spiritual healing was sealed in the Cross—the shed blood of Jesus. So Isaiah declared, "Surely He has borne our griefs / And carried our sorrows; / Yet we esteemed Him stricken, / Smitten by God, and afflicted. / But He was wounded for our transgressions, / He was bruised for our iniquities; / The chastisement for our peace was upon Him, / And by His stripes we are healed" (Isa. 53:4–5; cf. Matt. 8:17; 1 Peter 2:24). This eternal, spiritual healing effected by Jesus' shed blood on the cross saved, healed, and delivered you from destruction and into eternal life.

When God doesn't heal now cannot address the issue of eternity. When Christ's blood washed you clean from sin, you were eternally saved, healed, and delivered. Regardless of what is happening *now* in your body in time and space, as a believer you are healed!

When God doesn't heal now does address the issue of your eternal healing being manifested physically in your body in time and space *now!* Let's be certain of this fact: All physical healings from God in time and space are temporary. Everyone that Jesus healed in the first century died. Everyone healed by God in every subsequent age died. Until Jesus returns, everyone healed physically by God will die. "And as it is appointed for men to die once, but after this the judgment" (Heb. 9:27).

God does nothing in eternity *that does not fulfill His will or purpose.* When God saved, healed, and delivered us in eternity through the shed blood of Jesus Christ, He did so to fulfill His will. So what is the purpose or will of God in saving and healing us eternally? We will not only live spiritually with Him for eternity, but He will also give us perfect, whole, and healed or healthy bodies for eternity (1 Cor. 15). God wills or desires in His purpose that all be eternally saved, healed, and delivered: "For this is good and acceptable in the sight of God our Savior, who desires all men to be saved and to come to the knowledge of the truth" (1 Tim. 2:3–4). So God wills to save us so that we might dwell with Him forever (John 3:15; 10:28; 14:1–4; 17:2; Rom. 6:23; 1 Tim. 6:19; Titus 1:2).

God does nothing in time *that does not fulfill His will or purpose.* Jesus was very clear about this. He said or did nothing in time and space until God the Father did or said it (John 5:19ff.). God willed for the Hebrews to be freed from slavery in Egypt. He spoke His will to Moses, and He implemented His will in the Exodus. God willed for the Israelites to cross over the Jordan into the promised land. He spoke His will to Joshua, and He implemented His will as Israel crossed the Jordan on dry land.

THE PURPOSE OF PHYSICAL HEALING

Throughout the Bible, God did miraculous signs and wonders. What was the purpose of those signs and wonders? If we can understand the revealed purpose of God's mighty acts in history then we can begin to understand His revelation for us in healing. God's eternal healing doesn't manifest in time and space in random and capricious ways. He has a purpose behind all that He does in history.

The greatest miracle at the beginning of the Bible is creation. One of the words used for "miracle" in Scripture is *sign.* Obviously a sign points to something. Miracles are God's signposts purposefully pointing to something. What is that something? "The heavens declare the glory of God; / And the firmament shows His handiwork" (Ps. 19:1). The miraculous sign of creation points to God's glory.

Psalms 106–7 recount the mighty miracle of the Exodus for which the psalmist declares we should praise God and give Him thanks (106:48–107:1). When Mary learned of the Spirit's conception within her of the Messiah, she praised God (Luke 1:46ff.). Upon seeing the Christ child, the shepherds rejoiced and glorified God (Luke 2:20) as did Simeon and Anna (Luke 2:28, 38). When Jesus healed the ten lepers, only one understood the purpose of His healing: "So Jesus answered and said, 'Were there not ten cleansed? But where are the nine? Were there not any found who returned to give glory to God except this foreigner?'" (Luke 17:17–18). And when John recorded the purpose of Jesus' signs and miracles, he wrote, "This, the first of his miraculous signs, Jesus performed at Cana in Galilee. He thus revealed his glory, and his disciples put their faith in him" (John 2:11 NIV).

Perhaps no better example can be found than that of the crippled beggar whom God healed at the temple steps through Peter and John (Acts 3:1ff.). Once healed, the beggar went throughout the temple courtyard praising God and attracting great attention to Jesus. Peter declared, "It is Jesus' name and the faith that comes through him that has given this complete healing to him [the beggar], as you can all see" (Acts 3:16 NIV). Jesus received glory through healing. The lost were pointed to the saving power of Jesus Christ through healing.

When God heals *now*, He receives glory and honor. When God heals *now*, those who are healed praise and glorify the name of Jesus. When God heals *now,* the lost see a one-way sign pointing to the Savior.

God's will and purpose in healing *now* in time and space is this: to manifest His glory in Jesus Christ so that the lost will be saved. Up to this moment in time, you may have believed that your physical healing would be about you. Your healing is not about you; it's about God receiving glory so that those who are lost around you might be saved.

You may have bargained with God. Do any of these proposed deals sound familiar (you fill in the blank)?

- If You will just heal me, I will stop doing
  _____.

- If You will just heal me, I will serve You by doing
  _____.

- If You will just heal me, I will give You the glory and I will _____.

Deals are rationalizations and denials of reality; deals are the cousins of myths. To confront the deals, ask yourself these questions:

- If God doesn't heal me *now,* will I continue to do whatever it is I should not be doing?
- If I'm not serving Him when I am ill, why would I serve Him healed?
- If I am not glorifying Him for my eternal salvation, healing, and deliverance, why would I glorify Him in a temporary physical healing?

CHRONOS AND CHAIROS

Two Greek words describe time. *Chronos* is the normal, everyday passing of time—twenty-four hours a day, seven days a week. *Chairos* is a critical moment in time when the eternal invades the temporal. A *chairos,* or crisis, occurs when God's Spirit invades time to save, heal, and deliver.

When God heals *now,* a crisis occurs in your personal history. At that moment of physical healing, God's glory is manifested so that others will witness His salvation in Jesus Christ.

Until *chairos* happens in your life, you live with *chronos.* The ordinary passage of time is filled with one event after another. Every event in *chronos* has three elements: a cause, a result, and your response. The only variable in these three elements is *your response.*

A destructive virus or bacteria attacks your body. The result is illness. What is *your response?*

Your doctor runs a battery of tests and discovers disease in your body—heart disease, cancer, diabetes, hearing loss, arthritis, etc. Something has caused that disease—an attack of the enemy or a destructive life habit you may have. What is *your response?*

I am not asking what you might do to seek your healing. In a later chapter we will explore the action steps you may take when seeking a physical healing. *Response* precedes action. *Your response is your heart attitude toward God.*

There are two ways that *chairos* happens. One way is that God initiates . . . God acts. Supernaturally, God moves into history and manifests His glory and power. The second way is that when we experience whatever may happen in *chronos,* we *respond* with praise, thanksgiving, rejoicing, and praising God and open a door for *chairos*.

Jesus was looking for such a response from Martha at the tomb of Lazarus. Martha and the rest of the crowd were responding wrongly to the death of Lazarus. They had thought, *If only Jesus had come now and healed now, Lazarus would not have died.* But Jesus said to Martha, "Did I not say to you that if you would believe you would see the *glory* of God?" (John 11:40, emphasis added).

When was the glory of God manifested in the healing of Lazarus? When Jesus thanked the Father, and when Jesus revealed that the healing was not for Lazarus but for the benefit of the unbelievers gathered at the tomb (cf. John 11:41f.). This opened the door in *chronos* for the invasion of *chairos*. Chronos *is transformed into* chairos *when God is thanked, praised, and glorified.*

Permit me to ask you a meddlesome question in response to a common inquiry about healing. Some ask, "How is it that some are healed and some are not healed when we pray?" The more profound question might be, "How many are not healed because we have not prayed, praised, and thanked God for their healing even before it's manifested?"

We don't glorify God to be healed; we glorify Christ because we are healed eternally and forever *by His stripes.* And should God in His sovereign mercy purpose our healing *now,* then we simply have but one more event in time for which to give Him praise:

For *all things* are for your sakes, that grace, having spread through the many, may cause thanksgiving to abound to the glory of God. Therefore we do not lose heart. Even though our outward man is perishing, yet the inward man is being renewed day by day. For our light affliction, which is but for a moment, is working for us a far more exceeding and eternal weight of glory, while we do not look at the things which are seen, but at the things which are not seen. For the things which are seen are temporary, but the things which are not seen are eternal. (2 Cor. 4:15–18, emphasis added)

All things include being healed now and not being healed now.

When God doesn't heal *now,* give Him thanks, knowing that He works in all things "for the good of those who love him, who have been called according to his purpose" (Rom. 8:28 NIV).

When God doesn't heal *now,* "rejoice in the Lord always. I will say it again: Rejoice!" (Phil. 4:4 NIV).

When God doesn't heal *now,* transform your time into eternity by giving thanks to Him. "O LORD my God, I will give you thanks forever" (Ps. 30:12 NIV).

When God doesn't heal *now,* offer up the sacrifice of praise continually. "By Him let us continually offer the sacrifice of praise to God, that is, the fruit of our lips, giving thanks to His name" (Heb. 13:15).

HEALING AND GOD'S GLORY

In March of 1998, my wife and I flew to Baroda, India, to observe and write about a crusade and pastors' training meeting conducted by Peter Youngren, an evangelist and pastor from St. Catharines, Ontario, Canada.

On the second night of the crusade, I entered the Methodist compound grounds not as someone on the crusade team, but as an observer in the crowd. Peter preached a moving, evangelistic message about Jesus being the only man who had ever died and been raised from the dead and was now in our midst. When Peter Youngren proclaimed that Jesus was alive in our midst and able to heal the sick, give sight to the blind, make the lame walk and the deaf hear, God's healing power surged through a crowd of more than twenty thousand Indians in that place, most of whom were Hindus. As healings began to manifest everywhere in the crowd, those who were healed pushed forward. I wrote a description of what happened then:

Falling back to the sidelines, the police gave way to a rushing throng of healed children, teenagers, and adults. The altar filled with living testimonies of the saving and healing power of God.

A two-year-old girl, mute from birth, spoke her first words from a loosed tongue, "Hallelujah! Papa, Mama," she said over and over again as tears streamed down her grateful parents' faces. Peter told the crowd what she said, and thousands erupted in shouts of triumph and joy.

"Look over here—" Peter motioned to the right of the platform. "A young boy is dancing. Why is he dancing?" An usher shouted up the report from the boy's mother.

"He has had polio since birth and was barely able to walk. Now he dances completely healed by Jesus," Peter reported to a cheering crowd.

Above his head, a man wildly waved a pair of glasses with thick lenses made for those with cataracts. The old man's left eye gazed at my face without his glasses while his right eye remained locked shut from years of disuse.

I went with an interpreter to hear the man's story. "He says that he couldn't see at all in his right eye, and he could barely see things in front of his face with his left eye," the interpreter excitedly narrated. I backed away from the man a few feet and lifted my fingers. "How many fingers am I holding up?" I asked him, raising two fingers. He shouted "two" in Gujarati and held up two fingers as well. We played this game for a few minutes. Everyone around including the healed man was convinced that he could really see.

As I moved toward him and stood right in front of his face to see this miracle, I suddenly saw his previously closed right eye spring open, and, before my amazed stare, his cornea, which had been completely clouded with a severe cataract, cleared from obtuse to transparent in a matter of seconds. To my astonishment, both his eyes were now not only crystal clear but also blue as a noonday, cloudless sky. *Why blue?* I wondered. *Just as a newborn baby's eyes,* replied the Holy Spirit.

Giving God praise for the healings, Peter Youngren began leading the Indian congregation in a chorus of "Hallelu, Hallelu," with everyone in sight dancing joyfully before the Lord. Scores of others who had been healed pressed in to the ushers who were writing down the healing as quickly as they could. As the throngs began to leave the compound, each person was given a booklet with the salvation message of Jesus Christ written in his or her native tongue of Gujarati or Hindi.[12]

When God's healing power invades time and space, even the unsaved give glory to God and many who witness God's healing are saved.

When God heals now, give Him glory.
When God doesn't heal now, give Him glory!

Our prayers make a difference to God because of the
personal relationship
God enters into with us.
God chooses to make himself dependent on us for
certain things.
It is God's sovereign choice to establish this sort of
relationship; it is not forced on God by us.
                                        —JOHN SANDERS,
                                        The God Who Risks

CHAPTER 8

GOD'S SOVEREIGNTY

Two issues confront us when God doesn't heal now: God's timing is one; God's sovereignty is the other. To call God sovereign is to recognize His kingship. Earlier in this book we identified the three essential elements in Jesus' ministry: proclaiming the kingdom of God, healing, and deliverance. All three are inextricably intertwined.

Obviously, one cannot speak of a kingdom without focusing on the king. The Old Testament abounds with references describing God as King.

- "For God is the King of all the earth; / sing to him a psalm of praise" (Ps. 47:7 NIV).

- "Your procession has come into view, O God, / the procession of my God and King into the sanctuary" (Ps. 68:24 NIV).

- "I will extol You, my God, O King; / And I will bless Your name forever and ever" (Ps. 145:1).

- "But the LORD is the true God; / He is the living God and the everlasting King. / At His wrath the earth will tremble, / And the nations will not be able to endure His indignation" (Jer. 10:10).

In the New Testament, Jesus Christ is also designated as King.

- "That you keep this commandment without spot, blameless until our Lord Jesus Christ's appearing, which He will manifest in His own time, He who is the blessed and only Potentate, the King of kings and Lord of lords" (1 Tim. 6:14–15).

- "These will make war with the Lamb, and the Lamb will overcome them, for He is Lord of lords and King of kings; and those who are with Him are called, chosen, and faithful" (Rev. 17:14).

Being a sovereign implies four important things:

1. *Ownership.* The Hebrew word for "my Lord" (*adonai*) and the Greek word for "Lord" (*kyrios*) connote that everything belongs to God—the earth, the heavens, all wealth, and of course, God's people, the citizens of His kingdom.

2. *Authority.* As King, God has the absolute right to execute His will over His kingdom and all His subjects. His will is never arbitrary or capricious and always expresses His character as expressed in His righteousness and holy love. His absolute authority demands obedience from His people.

3. *Control.* God is in control. At times He is displeased

and may even express His wrath, but He cannot be manipulated or intimidated.

4. *Redemption.* God alone saves. "Divine sovereignty appears most clearly in redemption . . . Scripture highlights this sovereignty in several different ways . . . It constantly ascribes our salvation to God's mercy."[1]

Myths about healing tempt us to believe that healing depends on us, on others, or upon spiritual or religious rites and traditions. The truth is simply this: *Healing rests solely within the sovereignty of God's mercy.* Paul wrote, "For he [God] says to Moses, 'I will have mercy on whom I have mercy, / and I will have compassion on whom I have compassion.' It does not, therefore, depend on man's desire or effort, but on God's mercy" (Rom. 9:15–16 NIV; cf. Ex. 33:19).

WHY DOES GOD HEAL?

Now we are prepared to ask, Why does God heal? We can answer this question without conjuring up myths or trying to reason answers. Let's review what we have already discovered:

- While faith helps us to receive healing, God doesn't heal because of our faith. Faith never heals.

- While prayer opens the door to healing, God doesn't heal because we pray. Prayer never heals.

- While sin may hinder our healing, God doesn't punish us by not healing. God is always ready and able to heal.

- While healing may flow through someone touching or laying hands on us, a person's touch never heals.

Healing is rooted in the nature and character of God. He is the God who Heals. Out of His mercy and loving compassion for us, God heals. Lamentations declares this truth so plainly:

> Through the LORD'S mercies we are not consumed,
> Because His compassions fail not.
> They are new every morning;
> Great is Your faithfulness.
> "The LORD is my portion," says my soul,
> "Therefore I hope in Him!"
> The LORD is good to those who wait for Him,
> To the soul who seeks Him.
> It is good that one should hope and wait quietly
> For the salvation of the LORD. (Lam. 3:22–26)

Throughout the Gospels, we observe that Jesus was moved to heal out of mercy and compassion. Out of compassion, Jesus healed: "Then Jesus, moved with compassion, stretched out His hand and touched him, and said to him, 'I am willing; be cleansed'" (Mark 1:41; cf. Mark 5:19; 9:22; Luke 7:13). The Greek word for "compassion" (*splagchnizomai*) is the same word used in Romans 9:15 when God says, "I will have compassion on whomever I will have compassion." Healing flows from God's sovereign mercy and compassion.

When God heals *now*, He manifests His mercy. God's eternal mercy never ceases, but the manifestation of His mercy in time and space is always determined by His sovereignty.

When hundreds of people call upon God's mercy for healing in a healing crusade and some are healed now and some are not healed now, what answer can we give? *God's sovereignty.* Some may protest that such an answer is not comforting, but if I am uncomfortable with God's sovereignty, I have chosen to respond negatively instead of positively. God's comfort is freely given to all who seek it: "Praise be to the God and Father of our Lord Jesus Christ, the Father of compassion and the God of all comfort, who comforts us in all our troubles, so that we can comfort those in any trouble with the comfort we ourselves have received from God. For just as the sufferings of Christ flow over into our lives, so also through Christ our comfort overflows" (2 Cor. 1:3–5 NIV).

You may protest that you would rather be healed than comforted. The choice is not yours. His mercy and compassion are always manifested in time and space through His comfort. Why? Because God in compassion and mercy has sovereignly decided to do so. Physical healing may be manifested in time and space. Why? The same reason—because God in compassion and mercy has sovereignly decided to manifest it.

Consider some biblical examples of this. Jesus undoubtedly passed by the crippled beggar on the temple steps often during His ministry. He sovereignly chose not to heal him those times. But when Peter and John passed the beggar, God sovereignly healed the beggar. Was Jesus any less compassionate by not healing the beggar *now*? Of course not.

Jesus compassionately healed the paralytic at the pool of Bethesda. What about the other sick people around the pool? Jesus was also compassionate toward them but chose not to heal them physically *now*. We may offer many different reasons why Jesus did not heal *now*. But we can never be fully certain that any of those reasons can answer why Jesus didn't heal *now* except one—He is sovereign.

DOES ANYTHING I DO OR SAY MATTER?

If God is sovereign and He alone chooses when to heal *now*, can I do or say anything that will ultimately influence God to heal me *now*? Does faith make a difference? Does prayer? Does repentance? Does laying on of hands or anointing with oil? Does anything make a difference with God? The answer is irrevocably *yes!*

Our sovereign, compassionate God, the God who Heals, is also the God who Risks! God risks relationship with us. He exposes Himself to rejection and misunderstanding. God risks the possibility that we will break covenant with Him. His will as it is expressed in time and space comes to us with an invitation, "Come now, and let us reason together," / Says the LORD, / "Though your sins are like scarlet, / They shall be as white as snow; / Though they are red like crimson, / They shall be as wool" (Isa. 1:18).

In His sovereignty, God has expressed that His *perfect will* is for us to be saved and sanctified (1 Tim. 2:3ff.; 1 Thess. 4:3ff.). God's *permissive will* allows us to choose whom we will serve in this life—God or man (Josh. 24:15; Matt. 6:24ff.). God's *participatory will* invites us to participate with Him in making decisions and effecting His will in time and space (cf. Ex. 32–33; Isa. 1:18; Phil. 2:12ff.; 3:7–16).

John Sanders discussed the sovereignty of God regarding his participatory will in these terms:

The survey of biblical materials showed that God enters into genuine give-and-take relations with humans; what God wants does not always come about. The description of the divine nature as loving, wise, faithful and almighty promotes thinking of divine sovereignty in terms of general sovereignty, in which God chooses to macromanage most things while leaving open the option of micromanaging some things. This was God's sovereign choice. In grace God grants humans a role in collaborating with him on the course that human history takes. God provides "space" for us to operate and in so doing makes it possible that some of the specific goals he would like to see fulfilled may not come about. Nonetheless, God graciously works with us, being creatively resourceful, to achieve his overall project of establishing loving relationship with significant others. God is yet working with us to open up new possibilities for the future. God faithfully works toward his overarching goals while remaining flexible as to how he brings these about.[2]

We cannot control or manipulate our sovereign God. Faith, prayer, repentance, and claiming the promises of God do not force Him to act. But God has sovereignly chosen in His mercy and compassion to risk relationship with us in time and space. He has chosen to respond as He wills to faith, prayer, repentance, and acting upon His promises.

Let's return briefly to one biblical example we discussed earlier in this book. God spoke through the prophet Isaiah to King Hezekiah that the king would die (2 Kings 20:1ff.). Yet in response to Hezekiah's prayer, God sovereignly decided to heal him physically and allow the king to live another fifteen years. When God announced to King Hezekiah through the prophet Isaiah that he would die very soon, Hezekiah prayed and gave God reasons why He [God] should let him live longer. Because of his prayer God sent Isaiah back to Hezekiah to inform him that God had changed His mind and would grant his request (2 Kings 20:1–6). If Hezekiah had not prayed to God, biblical history would have been different. To modify James's statement: "They received because they asked. In the risk model it is quite possible for us to miss a blessing that God desires to give because we fail to ask for it (James 4:2–3)."[3] God sovereignly chose to respond to Hezekiah's prayer.

Therefore, in our relationship with God, we can seek His healing knowing that His decision to heal *now* does not depend on us but on Him. Of this we can be assured: God loves us; God has sovereignly decided to make some of His actions in time and space contingent upon our response to His love; God allows for us to work *with* Him in fulfilling His will and purpose for our lives; and God has granted us freedom to love Him in a give-and-take relationship. "In summary, God freely enters into genuine give-and-take relations with us. This entails risk taking on his part because we are capable of letting God down. This understanding of divine providence deeply affects our views concerning salvation, suffering and evil, prayer and divine guidance."[4]

Knowing that the God who Heals is the God who Risks, we can now begin to complete the sentence, *When God doesn't heal now* . . . In the concluding parts of this book, we will explore these completions as ways for us to respond to God:

When God doesn't heal *now*, walk through the valleys with faith.

When God doesn't heal *now,* pray with all kinds of prayer.

When God doesn't heal *now,* know, claim, and stand on God's promises.

When God doesn't heal *now,* face illness and the possibility of physical death with hope and victory.

When God doesn't heal *now,* there are ways for you to respond that will praise and glorify God. It's time to turn to those responses.

For we walk by faith, not by sight. We are confident, yes, well pleased rather to be absent from the body and to be present with the Lord. Therefore we make it our aim, whether present or absent, to be well pleasing to Him.

—PAUL THE APOSTLE,
2 Corinthians 5:7–9

CHAPTER 9

GOD'S WAY:
WALKING BY FAITH

When God doesn't heal *now,* walk by faith. Yes, God in His sovereignty may choose to heal *now* or you may walk through death's stingless portals into His everlasting arms. "The eternal God is your refuge, / And underneath are the everlasting arms; / He will thrust out the enemy from before you, / And will say, 'Destroy!'" (Deut. 33:27).

At the beginning of this book, I shared with you two stories. Rob and Joani suddenly found themselves in a life-threatening trauma. Joani's headache turned into a medical nightmare in which all of her organs began to shut down, and life support was her only link to physical life. Nonetheless, Rob doggedly walked by faith. He saw the invisible that was not yet and believed for it *now.* In the midst of their courageous walk of faith, God sovereignly chose to heal Joani physcially *now.*

In our second story, William and Alicia learned that she had medically incurable liver cancer. They committed themselves to walk by faith and not by sight. With courage and

131

indefatigable hope they walked together in time and space until Alicia stepped over into eternal life. Both couples were saved—healed eternally by His stripes. Both couples saw God respond to their faith and prayers in different ways. Both went through the valley of shadows victorious. "Yea, though I walk through the valley of the shadow of death, / I will fear no evil; / For You are with me; / Your rod and Your staff, they comfort me" (Ps. 23:4).

When our response to illness is to walk by faith, then the One we trust—the God who Heals—will never leave or forsake us (Heb. 13:5ff.). Until God heals *now* or we step over from time to eternity, how shall we walk by faith? The following four truths will strengthen you for your journey of faith.

TRUTH 1: VISIBLE FACTS ARE NOT TOTAL REALITY

A physician may tell you that your test results indicate that you have breast cancer, or heart disease, or diabetes, or another destructive disease. Some healing myths may tempt you to say that the disease really isn't there so you shouldn't speak it; you should instead deny its existence in time and space.

YOUR BATTLE IS NOT AGAINST DISEASE

Whatever attack of illness you or a loved one may be facing is not your destiny or purpose in life. You were not born to have this disease. Your purpose in life is not to fight the battle against disease and death. That battle belongs to the

Lord (1 Sam. 17:47), and He has already won it (Rom. 8:28–39; 1 Cor. 15:54–58). By faith you can grasp the total reality, which is both visible and invisible. Hebrews 11:1–3 proclaims, "Now faith is being sure of what we hope for and certain of what we do not see. This is what the ancients were commended for. By faith we understand that the universe was formed at God's command, so that what is seen was not made out of what was visible" (NIV).

The greatest battle you will fight will be against fear. God knows that. In fact, more than one hundred times in Scripture God says in various ways to us, "Fear not." Fear does not come from God but from the world and Satan. Satan's design is to tempt you to replace faith with fear. The world responds to frightening facts with fear instead of faith. Not so for believers—they respond to fearsome facts with awesome faith. Such faith flies in the face of temporal events with the eternal truth: "For God has not given us a spirit of fear, but of power and of love and of a sound mind" (2 Tim. 1:7). Reason may say, "Fear," but faith says, "That's irrational. With my sound mind, I have God's power and love to endure and overcome any trial or tribulation in life."

REBUKE FEAR

Fear causes us to irrationally think that the trials and tribulations of disease will destroy our faith. In fact, the opposite is truth. Trials and tribulations strengthen and refine faith.

In this you greatly rejoice, though now for a little while, if need be, you have been grieved by various trials, that the genuineness of your faith, being much more precious than gold that perishes, though it is tested by fire, may be found to praise, honor, and glory at the revelation of Jesus Christ, whom having not seen you love. Though now you do not see Him, yet believing, you rejoice with joy inexpressible and full of glory, receiving the end of your faith—the salvation of your souls. (1 Peter 1:6–9)

FIX YOUR FAITH ON TRUTH

When you fix your eyes of faith on Jesus, then your responses will be directed by truth, not by facts or circumstances. Your illness cannot become the center of your life or the focus of your attention. If it does, then you will find yourself on an emotional roller coaster with every medical report or physical pain determining how you feel. Don't surrender control of your life or your feeling to your disease. Surrender yourself to the anchor of hope—Jesus Christ. Your hope will remain constant because Truth never changes—only facts change. Jesus, the Truth (John 14:6), is the same yesterday, today, and forever (Heb. 13:8). And your faith will grow stronger and deeper as you walk with Christ through every trial and test (James 1:12–18).

TRUTH 2: FAITH WALKING
IS PRAYER WALKING

Prayer sustains and builds your walk of faith through pain, suffering, and trial. Effective prayer patiently petitions God and waits on Him. Waiting does not imply passivity. Do all you can do in the natural to strengthen your physical body with good nutrition, helpful medical treatment, exercise, and a positive mental outlook.

Waiting does mean that you trust God and do not tempt Him (James 1:12ff.). Tempting God is a bargaining, deal-making relationship in which you make promises to God out of desperation instead of love. A trusting relationship asks God for what you need and waits on His answer. "My brethren, take the prophets, who spoke in the name of the Lord, as an example of suffering and patience. Indeed we count them blessed who endure. You have heard of the perseverance of Job and seen the end intended by the Lord—that the Lord is very compassionate and merciful" (James 5:10–11). God will supply your needs and sovereignly answer your prayers (Phil. 4:4–19).

In your walk of faith, keep a prayer journal. Daily memorize, meditate on, and apply God's Word to your life. Like medicine, His Word brings healing (Ps. 107:20; Prov. 4:20–22). Daily pray for the needs of others and then your needs (Matt. 21:22; Eph. 6:18). Daily thank, praise, and give God glory for His nature, compassion, mercy, grace, and love. Praise Him for Christ's finished work of redemption on the cross—saving, healing, and delivering you by His shed blood. Glorify His name for all the signs and wonders He has wrought in your life. Tell God how much you love Him with your whole heart, body, mind, soul, and strength. And when you don't know how to pray, ask the Spirit to intercede for you (Rom. 8:26–27).

The verses you choose to meditate on can be selected from the passages discussed in the next chapter. Following is a journal page you may copy for your use.

DAILY IN GOD'S HEALING WORD

Date:_____   Text:_____

Healing Scripture:_____

_____

_____

Prayer for the needs of others:_____

_____

_____

Prayer for your needs:_____

_____

_____

Signs, wonders, and answered prayers for which you glorify, praise, and thank God:_____

_____

_____

Tell God the Father, Son, and Spirit how much you love Him:

_____

_____

_____

Listen to God's voice. Write down what He is saying to you:

_____

_____

_____

Ask the Holy Spirit to intercede for those things for which you do not know how to pray:_____

_____

_____

Notes:_____

_____

TRUTH 3: GOD AND HIS WORD
CAN BE TRUSTED

Faith takes God at His Word and trusts His compassion and mercy. Take time to read carefully Psalm 119. The benefits of God's Word are detailed for you and will encourage you as you trust His Word. When you cannot see His hand, trust His Word. At times, you will not be able to understand *why* God is allowing events to take a certain direction, and you may become frustrated or impatient. When God doesn't heal *now*, trust His word and wait upon Him. Deposit these two Scriptures into your spirit:

- "But those who wait on the LORD / Shall renew their strength; / They shall mount up with wings like eagles, / They shall run and not be weary, / They shall walk and not faint" (Isa. 40:31).

- "For all the promises of God in Him are Yes, and in Him Amen, to the glory of God through us. Now He who establishes us with you in Christ and has anointed us is God, who also has sealed us and given us the Spirit in our hearts as a guarantee" (2 Cor. 1:20–22).

Faith knows all there is to know and does all that can be done in the natural. Dr. Cherry wrote about important principles for acting in faith, trusting God to guide us in His pathway to healing:

1. God has a specific pathway that will lead to your healing.

2.   You must pray and seek God for that pathway.

3.   God uses both the natural and the supernatural to heal.

4.   All the healings that Jesus performed under that old covenant were effected on the basis of what He was going to do on Calvary when He established a new covenant.

5.   After you do what you can do in the natural, God will act in the supernatural to provide for your healing.

6.   God provided a detailed plan of nutrition for His people.

7.   As a Christian, you have power and authority over disease through the blood of Jesus Christ.

8.   You can take authority over sickness and disease in your body by seeing, reading, speaking, and hearing God's Word.[1]

TRUTH 4: FAITH FOCUSES ON THE HEALER, NOT THE HEALING

Finally, the focus of your faith should be Jesus Christ, your Healer. How often I've heard people say, "I'm believing for my healing." Instead, their confession needed to be, "I'm trusting Jesus, my Healer."

Whenever we concentrate on what we expect Jesus to give us or do for us, we will create a myth to comfort us and build an idol to help us. In fact, our healing can block our vision. We become so shortsighted in wanting to be healed *now* that we lose sight of the Lord whom we trust and follow. I know people who chase healing evangelists all over the world trying to "get their healing." What sad lives they live. Alway disappointed, forever frustrated, constantly drained of emotion and money, they are like ships adrift, blown around helplessly by winds of doubt, fear, and unbelief. They become double-minded:

> My brethren, count it all joy when you fall into various trials, knowing that the testing of your faith produces patience. But let patience have its perfect work, that you may be perfect and complete, lacking nothing. If any of you lacks wisdom, let him ask of God, who gives to all liberally and without reproach, and it will be given to him. But let him ask in faith, with no doubting, for he who doubts is like a wave of the sea driven and tossed by the wind. For let not that man suppose that he will receive anything from the Lord; he is a double-minded man, unstable in all his ways. (James 1:2–8)

Walking by faith in Christ results in two powerful attitudes:

1. You will never quit!
2. You will finish strong!

As Paul reflected on his life, he had matured to the attitude that you are developing as you walk by faith:

Yet indeed I also count all things loss for the excellence of the knowledge of Christ Jesus my Lord, for whom I have suffered the loss of all things, and count them as rubbish, that I may gain Christ and be found in Him, not having my own righteousness, which is from the law, but that which is through faith in Christ, the righteousness which is from God by faith; that I may know Him and the power of His resurrection, and the fellowship of His sufferings, being conformed to His death, if, by any means, I may attain to the resurrection from the dead. Not that I have already attained, or am already perfected; but I press on, that I may lay hold of that for which Christ Jesus has also laid hold of me. Brethren, I do not count myself to have apprehended; but one thing I do, forgetting those things which are behind and reaching forward to those things which are ahead, I press toward the goal for the prize of the upward call of God in Christ Jesus. Therefore let us, as many as are mature, have this mind; and if in anything you think otherwise, God will reveal even this to you. Nevertheless, to the degree that we have already attained, let us walk by the same rule, let us be of the same mind. Brethren, join in following my example, and note those who so walk, as you have us for a pattern. For many walk, of whom I have told you often, and now tell you even weeping, that they are the enemies of the cross of Christ: whose end is destruction, whose god is their belly, and whose glory is in their shame—who set their mind on earthly things. For our citizenship is in heaven, from which we also eagerly wait for the Savior, the Lord Jesus Christ, who will transform our lowly body that it may be conformed to His glorious body, according to the working by which He is able even to subdue all things to Himself.

—(Phil. 3:8–21)

CHAPTER 10

GOD'S HEALING WORD

Memorizing, meditating, singing, speaking, and praying God's Word as you walk by faith will strengthen you physically and spiritually. The following biblical passages contain many of the great healing verses of the Bible and wonderful promises of God that can be applied for your healing through the blood and name of the Lord Jesus Christ.

Each passage is quoted from the New King James Version, which is an excellent translation for committing His truth to memory. In Scripture, numbers often convey a spiritual meaning. The number 40 commonly refers to a period of trial or tribulation that your sickness may be for your life.

Take these forty steps as you walk by faith through your wilderness of testing and into God's healing compassion and grace. With each Scripture I have included two or three action points and a prayer that prays that Scripture. It's important not only to say it but also to pray it. Praying God's Word powerfully speaks defeat to any physical attack against you and also speaks victory over the disease in you. To apply His Word as medicine for your healing, take these steps:

STEP 1: *PRAY FOR HEALING*

"So Abraham prayed to God; and God healed Abimelech, his wife, and his female servants. Then they bore children" (Gen. 20:17).

- Pray without ceasing.
- Pray persistently.
- Pray with thanksgiving.
- Pray expectantly.
- Pray in faith.

Lord, I lift my prayer to You for healing. Amen.

STEP 2: *OBEY THE VOICE OF THE GOD WHO HEALS*

"And [the Lord] said, 'If you diligently heed the voice of the LORD your God and do what is right in His sight, give ear to His commandments and keep all His statutes, I will put none of the diseases on you which I have brought on the Egyptians. For I am the LORD who heals you'" (Ex. 15:26).

- Obey God's written Word in Scripture.
- Obey God's voice as He speaks to you by His Spirit.
- Obey God even when your circumstances seem to contradict His Word.
- Obey God's voice, not human voices.

- Obey God by crucifying self and pride, abandoning yourself totally to His will.

O God who Heals, I ask for Your Spirit to empower my obedience that I might walk in Your divine healing. Amen.

STEP 3: CRY OUT TO GOD FOR YOUR HEALING

"So Moses cried out to the LORD, saying, 'Please heal her, O God, I pray!'" (Num. 12:13).

- Cry out with a loud voice.
- Cry out with tears of repentance.
- Cry out with a broken and contrite heart.
- Cry out for God's mercy and compassion.

Heal me now, O God, I beseech You. Amen.

STEP 4: TRUST GOD ALONE AS THE SOURCE OF YOUR HEALING

"Now see that I, even I, am He, / And there is no God besides Me; / I kill and I make alive; / I wound and I heal; / Nor is there any who can deliver from My hand" (Deut. 32:39).

- Trust God, not human wisdom, for your healing.
- Trust God to be with you even when He doesn't heal *now*.

- Trust God to reveal your pathway to healing both in the natural and supernatural.

- Trust God to deliver you from physical attacks.

- Trust God to protect you from the enemy.

Lord, deliver me from the enemy. Make me alive by Your Spirit. Amen.

STEP 5: REPENT AND ASK FOR HIS HEALING FORGIVENESS

"So they said, 'If you send away the ark of the God of Israel, do not send it empty; but by all means return it to Him with a trespass offering. Then you will be healed, and it will be known to you why His hand is not removed from you'" (1 Sam. 6:3).

- Repent for all past sins of omission and commission.

- Repent for holding any offenses against others.

- Repent for unforgiveness in your heart.

- Repent and break any curse for the sins of previous generations in your family.

Lord, I repent of my sins of omission and commission. I repent of offenses in my heart against others. I forgive those who have sinned against me. And in Jesus' name I break every curse from the past on me or my family. Amen.

STEP 6: *ASK THE LORD TO HEAL THE DRY AND BARREN PLACES IN YOUR LIFE WITH HIS RIVERS OF LIVING WATERS*

"Then he went out to the source of the water, and cast in the salt there, and said, 'Thus says the LORD: "I have healed this water; from it there shall be no more death or barrenness"'" (2 Kings 2:21).

- Ask God's spirit to reveal the dry places.
- Pray to be filled and overflowing with His living water that renews and refreshes.

Lord, heal the dry and barren places in my life. Spring up, O Well of Life within me, from the One who gives His living water that I may never thirst again. Amen.

STEP 7: *GO INTO THE HOUSE OF THE LORD AND BE HEALED*

"Return and tell Hezekiah the leader of My people, 'Thus says the LORD, the God of David your father: "I have heard your prayer, I have seen your tears; surely I will heal you. On the third day you shall go up to the house of the LORD"'" (2 Kings 20:5).

- Go to God's house when you are sick to worship and be in His presence.

- Go to God's house when you are sick to have others pray for and lay hands on you for healing.

- Go to God's house when you are sick, and do not isolate yourself by staying home.

- Go to God's house when you are sick, **and praise Him** for His goodness, mercy, and healing through the shed blood of Jesus.

Lord, I come to Your house for worship, service, and healing—but most of all to seek Your face. Amen.

STEP 8: *PRAY NOT ONLY FOR YOUR OWN HEALING BUT ALSO FOR HEALING IN THE LAND*

"If My people who are called by My name will humble themselves, and pray and seek My face, and turn from their wicked ways, then I will hear from heaven, and will forgive their sin and heal their land" (2 Chron. 7:14).

- Pray for the healing of others not just yourself.
- Pray for healing in your church.
- Pray for healing in the body of Christ.
- Pray for healing in your state, nation, and the world.

Lord, break my pride. Humble me. Heal others . . . my church . . . the body of Christ . . . and the world around me. Amen.

STEP 9: *PETITION YOUR LEADERS TO PRAY FOR YOUR HEALING*

"And the LORD listened to Hezekiah and healed the people" (2 Chron. 30:20).

- Petition your leaders to agree in prayer for your healing.

- Petition your leaders to anoint you with oil for healing.

- Petition your leaders to praise God for your healing.

Lord, I pray for my leaders and ask Your Spirit to prompt them to pray for me. Amen.

STEP 10: *SING, PRAY, AND DECLARE THESE PSALMS FOR YOUR HEALING:*

"Have mercy on me, O LORD, for I am weak; / O LORD, heal me, for my bones are troubled" (Ps. 6:2).

"O LORD my God, I cried out to You, / And You healed me" (Ps. 30:2).

"I said, 'LORD, be merciful to me; / Heal my soul, for I have sinned against You'" (Ps. 41:4).

"Who forgives all your iniquities, / Who heals all your diseases" (Ps. 103:3).

"He sent His word and healed them, / And delivered them from their destructions" (Ps. 107:20).

- Praise God for your healing.

- Praise God for healing others.

- Praise God for His promise to heal.

- Praise God for the Word He sent forth in healing.

O Lord, have mercy on me for I am weak. Forgive my sin. Send forth Your word to heal me. Amen.

STEP 11: SEEK GOD'S TIMING FOR YOUR HEALING

"A time to kill, / And a time to heal; / A time to break down, / And a time to build up" (Eccl. 3:3).

- Be prepared. God's timing for healing includes both now and eternity.

- Seek God's will, in His timing, His way, and for His glory for your healing.

- Be patient. God's healing never arrives early or late. God is always on time.

Lord, reveal to me the timing of Your healing. Amen.

STEP 12: *ENJOY THE ABUNDANCE OF HIS HEALING*

"Behold I will bring it health and healing; I will heal them and reveal to them the abundance of peace and truth" (Jer. 33:6).

- Believe for God's healing abundance.

- Seek to understand His healing ways.
- Rejoice always in His healing.

Lord Jesus, I rebuke the enemy and demand back all that he destroyed and stole including my health. Lord, fill me with Your abundance. Amen.

STEP 13: *GOD HEALS EVERY WOUND*

"Moreover the light of the moon will be as the light of the sun, / And the light of the sun will be sevenfold, / As the light of seven days, / In the day that the LORD binds up the bruise of His people, / And heals the stroke of their wound" (Isa. 30:26).

- Expose every wound to God for healing.
- Let God heal every past hurt.
- Become a wounded healer ministering His healing to others.

O God, expose my wounds, my pain, and my hurt. Bind them up and heal me. Amen.

STEP 14: *BY HIS STRIPES, YOU ARE HEALED*

"But He was wounded for our transgressions, / He was bruised for our iniquities; / The chastisement for our peace was upon Him, / And by His stripes we are healed" (Isa. 53:5).

- Be cleansed and healed by the shed blood of Jesus.
- Pray and apply the blood for healing of others.
- Praise God that by Jesus' stripes you are healed.

Lord Jesus, how grateful I am that You were wounded for my transgressions and bruised for my iniquities. Heal my body, soul, and spirit by Your stripes. Amen.

STEP 15: *GOD SEES YOUR NEED AND WILL HEAL YOU*

"'I have seen his ways, and will heal him; / I will also lead him, / And restore comforts to him / And to his mourners. / I create the fruit of the lips: / Peace, peace to him who is far off and to him who is near,' / Says the LORD, / 'And I will heal him'" (Isa. 57:18–19).

- Give all your needs to Jesus.
- Receive God's peace as you await your healing in time and space.
- Know that the Lord is near to you.

Lord, examine my way. Meet my needs. Heal me. Grant me Your peace. Amen.

STEP 16: *YOUR HEALING IS SPEEDING YOUR WAY*

"Then your light shall break forth like the morning, / Your healing shall spring forth speedily, / And your righteousness shall go before you; / The glory of the LORD shall be your rear guard" (Isa. 58:8).

- Seek God's glory in your healing.
- Let His light burn brightly in your life.

As the dawn speedily ushers in the noonday sun, fill me, O God, with Your light that my healing might break forth as the sunrise and You might be glorified. Amen.

STEP 17: *THERE IS A BALM IN GILEAD—JESUS!*

"Is there no balm in Gilead, / Is there no physician there? / Why then is there no recovery / For the health of the daughter of my people?" (Jer. 8:22).

- Know that Jesus is the balm of your healing.
- Apply His anointing to the wounds of your heart.
- Let the Great Physician minister to you.

Balm of Gilead, be my Physician and pour the oil of Your healing on my body and soul. Amen.

STEP 18: *ASK THE LORD TO HEAL YOU*

"Heal me, O LORD, and I shall be healed; / Save me, and I shall be saved, / For You are my praise" (Jer. 17:14).

- Ask and expect to receive from the Lord.
- Make the Lord the object of your praise.
- Seek Him for your salvation and your healing.

Heal me, O Lord, and I shall be healed; save me, and I shall be saved: for You are my praise. Amen.

STEP 19: *GOD WILL RESTORE YOUR HEALTH*

"'For I will restore health to you / And heal you of your wounds,' says the LORD, / 'Because they called you an outcast saying: / "This is Zion; / No one seeks her"'" (Jer. 30:17).

"Behold, I will bring it health and healing; I will heal them and reveal to them the abundance of peace and truth" (Jer. 33:6).

- God cures and heals.
- Peace accompanies God's healing.

Almighty God, cure me and fill me with peace and truth. Amen.

STEP 20: *COME TO HIS LIVING WATERS AND BE HEALED*

"Then he said to me: 'This water flows toward the eastern region, goes down into the valley, and enters the sea. When it reaches the sea, its waters are healed'" (Ezek. 47:8).

"And it shall be that every living thing that moves, wherever the rivers go, will live. There will be a very great multitude of fish, because these waters go there; for they will be healed, and everything will live wherever the river goes" (Ezek. 47:9).

- The living water of the Holy Spirit refreshes and heals.

- Let the river of God's healing power flow through you.

Living water of God, flow in me, through me, and out of me. Amen.

STEP 21: *TURN TO THE LORD AND BE HEALED*

"Come, and let us return to the LORD; / For he has torn, but He will heal us; / He has stricken, but He will bind us up" (Hos. 6:1).

- If you have been distant from the Lord, it's time to return to Him.

- Find healing in the Lord.
- Returning to the Lord will bring healing to your brokenness and restoration to your relationships.

Lord, I return to You for my healing. Bind up my wounds. Amen.

STEP 22: *GOD'S SON OF RIGHTEOUSNESS, JESUS CHRIST, GOES BEFORE YOU WITH HEALING IN HIS WINGS*

"But to you who fear My name / The Sun of Righteousness shall arise / With healing in His wings; / And you shall go out / And grow fat like stall-fed calves" (Mal. 4:2).

- Follow His righteousness and be healed.
- Rise up from fearing disease and instead fear the Lord and be healed.

Christ, Sun of Righteousness, cover me with Your wings and heal me. Amen.

STEP 23: *WHATEVER YOUR SICKNESS, JESUS HEALS*

"Jesus went about all Galilee, teaching in their synagogues, preaching the gospel of the kingdom, and healing all kinds of sickness and all kinds of disease among the people" (Matt. 4:23).

- Take every disease and sickness to Jesus.
- Wherever you are physically or emotionally, He is willing to heal you.

Jesus, heal every disease in my body and set me free from sickness. Amen.

STEP 24: *FAITH IN JESUS BRINGS WHOLENESS*

"But Jesus turned around, and when He saw her He said, 'Be of good cheer daughter; your faith has made you well.' And the woman was made well from that hour" (Matt. 9:22).

- Faith in Jesus brings wholeness to your body.
- Faith in Jesus brings wholeness to your soul.
- Faith in Jesus brings wholeness to your spirit.

Jesus, by faith I come to You to be made whole. Amen.

STEP 25: *JESUS IS FILLED WITH COMPASSION FOR YOU*

"And when Jesus went out He saw a great multitude; and He was moved with compassion for them, and healed their sick" (Matt. 14:14).

- In this time of your disease, Jesus has compassion for you.

- Compassion is the reason Jesus heals.
- Be moved by compassion when you pray for others who are sick.

Lord Jesus, have mercy on me, and out of Your infinite compassion, heal me. Amen.

STEP 26: PRESS IN TO JESUS AND BE HEALED

"For He healed many, so that as many as had afflictions pressed about Him to touch Him" (Mark 3:10).

- Pressing in to Jesus brings a river of healing.
- Seek to touch Him in all that you seek.
- Remember that His touch is greater than your plague.

Lord, I am pressing in to touch You and be healed. Amen.

STEP 27: WHATEVER YOUR BONDAGE, JESUS WILL SET YOU FREE

"And they cast out many demons, and anointed with oil many who were sick, and healed them" (Mark 6:13).

- Jesus defeats every demonic attack.
- Ask the elders to anoint you with oil and pray for your healing.

O Bondage Breaker, set me free. Amen.

STEP 28: *TOUCH JESUS AND BE MADE WELL*

"Wherever He entered, into villages, cities, or the country, they laid the sick in the marketplaces, and begged Him that they might just touch the hem of His garment. And as many as touched Him were made well" (Mark 6:56).

- Reach out to touch Jesus for your healing.
- Push through every physical and spiritual obstacle to touch Jesus.
- Believe for your breakthrough to touch Him.

To touch You, Jesus, is my heartfelt desire. Amen.

STEP 29: *JESUS HEALS THE BROKENHEARTED*

"The Spirit of the LORD is upon Me, / Because He has anointed Me / To preach the gospel to the poor; / He has sent Me to heal the brokenhearted, / To proclaim liberty to the captives / And recovery of sight to the blind, / To set at liberty those who are oppressed" (Luke 4:18).

- Brokenhearted? Jesus heals.
- Bound up? Jesus heals.
- Blind? Jesus heals.
- Bruised and hurting? Jesus heals.

Anointed One, heal my broken heart, bind up my wounds, grant me sight, and deliver me from every bondage. Amen.

STEP 30: *JESUS IS COMING TO LAY HANDS ON YOU FOR YOUR HEALING*

"When the sun was setting, all those who had any that were sick with various diseases brought them to Him; and He laid His hands on every one of them and healed them" (Luke 4:40).

- Ask Jesus to lay hands on you for your healing.
- Take your disease to Jesus.
- Expect to be healed.

O Jesus, stretch forth Your hand and heal me. Amen.

STEP 31: *THE POWER OF THE LORD IS PRESENT TO HEAL YOU*

"Now it happened on a certain day, as He was teaching, that there were Pharisees and teachers of the law sitting by, who had come out of every town of Galilee, Judea, and Jerusalem. And the power of the Lord was present to heal them" (Luke 5:17).

- In His presence, you are healed.
- Seek His presence more than your healing.

Power of God, fall on me. Be present to heal me, O Lord. Amen.

STEP 32: *AT THE POINT OF DEATH?*
ONLY JESUS CAN HEAL YOU

"When he heard that Jesus had come out of Judea into Galilee, he went to Him and implored Him to come down and heal his son, for he was at the point of death" (John 4:47).

- Focus your requests on Jesus.

- Pray for His healing, comfort, and presence.

I seek You and You alone, O Christ, to be my Healer. Amen.

STEP 33: *ASK YOURSELF, "DO I REALLY*
WANT TO BE MADE WHOLE?"

"When Jesus saw him lying there, and knew that he already had been in that condition a long time, He said to him, 'Do you want to be made well?'" (John 5:6).

- Do you really want to be healed?

- Put aside all self-pity, depression, and doubt.

Forsaking all that would hold me back, I will to be made well by You, O Lord. Amen.

STEP 34: *ASK THE LORD TO STRETCH FORTH HIS HAND TO HEAL YOU*

"By stretching out Your hand to heal, and that signs and wonders may be done through the name of Your holy Servant Jesus" (Acts 4:30).

- Jesus is anointed to heal you.

"How God anointed Jesus of Nazareth with the Holy Spirit and with power, who went about doing good and healing all who were oppressed by the devil, for God was with Him" (Acts 10:38).

- His anointing heals.
- All that is good in my life comes from Jesus.

Lord Jesus, stretch forth Your healing hand to heal me by the power of Your anointing. Amen.

STEP 35: *SEEK OUT THOSE WITH THE GIFTS OF HEALING IN THE CHURCH TO PRAY FOR YOU*

"To another faith by the same Spirit, to another gifts of healings by the same Spirit" (1 Cor. 12:9).

- Ask God through the power of His Spirit to stir up gifts of healing all around you.
- Pray for the gifts of healing to manifest in your church.

Release Your healing gifts in our church, Spirit of God. Amen.

STEP 36: *IN OUR WEAKNESS, THE LORD IS STRONG*

"And He said to me, 'My grace is sufficient for you, for My strength is made perfect in weakness.' Therefore most gladly I will rather boast in my infirmities, that the power of Christ may rest upon me. Therefore I take pleasure in infirmities, in reproaches, in needs, in persecutions, in distresses, for Christ's sake. For when I am weak, then I am strong" (2 Cor. 12:9–10).

- Don't deny your illness or your weakness. Surrender it to Christ.
- Let Christ use your weaknesses to demonstrate His strength to others.

Christ, use my weakness as the broken vessel through which Your strength flows to others. Amen.

STEP 37: *PRAY FOR YOUR HEALING AND DO NOT WORRY*

"Be anxious for nothing, but in everything by prayer and supplication, with thanksgiving, let your requests be made known to God" (Phil 4:6).

"And my God shall supply all your need according to His riches in glory by Christ Jesus" (Phil. 4:19).

- Make a list of your needs and take them to Christ Jesus.

- Put aside your worry and pick up prayer.

- Give thanks in all things.

Christ, I give You my anxiety. Grant me the peace that passes all understanding. Supply my needs according to Your riches in glory. Amen.

STEP 38: *WALK IN YOUR HEALING*

"Therefore strengthen the hands which hang down, and the feeble knees, and make straight paths for your feet, so that what is lame may not be dislocated, but rather be healed" (Heb. 12:12–13).

- Walk in your healing.

- Decide to commit your every step in life to His leading and guidance.

I lift up heavy hands in praise and pray in faith on feeble knees. Make straight my paths, O God, that I might walk in Your healing. Amen.

STEP 39: *ASK THE ELDERS TO PRAY FOR YOU*

"Confess your trespasses to one another, and pray for one another, that you may be healed. The effective, fervent prayer of a righteous man avails much" (James 5:16).

- Confess sin immediately.

- Pray for others.

- Seek out the righteous to pray for you.

Lord, lead me to those to whom I will confess my sins. Prompt me to pray for those who are sick. Amen.

STEP 40: *PROSPER IN HEALTH*

"Beloved, I pray that you may prosper in all things and be in health, just as your soul prospers" (3 John 2).

- Declare God as your source.

- Know that all prosperity comes from Him.

- Walk in health by taking care of your body—the temple of the Holy Spirit.

O God, You are my source, my prosperity, and my health. Amen.

Your adversary would love for you to assume the worst about your situation.

He would enjoy seeing you heave a sigh and resign yourself to feelings of depression.

However, it's been my experience that when God is involved, anything can happen.

The One who directed that stone in between Goliath's eyes

and split the Red Sea down the middle

and leveled that wall around Jericho

and brought His Son back from beyond takes delight in mixing up the odds

as He alters the inevitable and bypasses the impossible.

The blind songwriter, Fanny Crosby, put it another way:

"Chords that were broken will vibrate once more."

—CHARLES R. SWINDOLL,
Encourage Me

When God Doesn't Heal *Now*, What's Next?

Who *you are* is far more important than *what you do*. Being precedes doing. If *who you are* isn't right, then *what you do* can never be the right thing to do.

And *who you are* is rooted in *whose you are*. Being proceeds out of belonging. Do you belong to yourself, your family, your church, your tradition, your body, your disease . . . or do you belong to Jesus?

When I interned as a hospital chaplain, I heard the nurses say, "The colon cancer in room #12 needs her medication. The biopsy in #14 needs a dressing changed. The heart cath in #20 needs his drip adjusted." People were identified by their problem or disease. Is that how you have allowed yourself to be known? Are you a cancer victim? Have you become a heart attack risk?

What was the defining moment for you in this attack of illness? Was it when you learned you were sick or when you gave your sickness to Christ? Was it when you faced your mortality for the first time? Or was it when you trusted Jesus for your immortality?

Yes, *who you are* right now will define *what you will do* when God doesn't heal *now*.

WHO YOU ARE IS DEFINED BY WHOSE YOU ARE

Do you belong to Jesus Christ? Paul wrote, "Or don't you know that your body is the temple of the Holy Spirit, who lives in you and was given to you by God? You do not belong to yourself, for God bought you with a high price. So you must honor God with your body" (1 Cor. 6:19–20 NLT).

If you do not belong to Jesus, then surrender yourself to Him right now. Pray this prayer:

Lord Jesus, I give You all of me—body, soul, and spirit. I surrender all. I repent of my sins and confess You, Jesus, as the Christ, the Son of the living God. I receive You as my personal Lord and Savior. Jesus, thank You for saving me and giving me the gift of eternal life and of the Holy Spirit. Amen.

Belonging to Jesus, you are now ready to do something. Being His, belonging to Christ and being filled with His Spirit, empowers you to walk by faith in these ways: When God doesn't heal *now*:

- Pray continually.
- Praise Him.
- Wait patiently upon Him in the passing of time (*chronos*).

- Seek Him to intervene in time *(chairos)* and heal you supernaturally.

- Surrender your life to His plan, purpose, and sovereign will for you.

- Read, recite, and rely on His Word, claiming all His promises for your life.

- Decide to live victoriously now and to never become a victim.

- Walk by faith.

Alicia's daughter shared these important insights for what to do when God doesn't heal *now*:

> I think it's important that we remember not to seek for healing but to seek the Healer. And I think that is what Mom did. She sought hard after Him every day. And we get so caught up in what God can do for us that we forget what He is to us. And I think that that's probably one of the most important things for somebody, even a family member or someone who is suffering, to not seek after what God can do for you but to seek after Him. 'Cause only there [in Him] are the answers. That's it!

Alicia died. Her healing miracle culminated in victory over death through eternal life, and her victory gave God glory. Through her living and dying many were led to Jesus. Joani was healed physically. Her healing miracle in time and space glorified God and led many to Jesus.

For Alicia, the last few days of her physical life were so painful that her eternal healing came as both a release from pain and a blessing. To her last breath, her family and friends all believed that God could heal her at any moment during her illness. They believed that God could raise her from the dead if He chose. They also trusted Him to choose her purpose and destiny for time and eternity. Do you trust the God who Heals with your life, both in time and eternity?

Take assurance and comfort in the truth that the God who Heals in time and eternity never leaves or forsakes you. I will never forget Joe. As a young pastor, I visited Joe and his family in the hospital. In the final days of a long terminal illness, Joe refused to give up hope for his healing, but he was quite willing to give up life for eternity whenever God called him home. His form of bone cancer filled his body with severe and constant pain. His doctors kept increasing his pain medication until he was at the point of sleeping most of the time. Soon he would enter a coma.

One evening, Joe and his family asked me if I would pray with them for God to heal Joe *now* or take him home to his eternal healing *now*. With a flood of tears, we all held hands and prayed together.

Joe's family was exhausted after having faithfully attended his bedside for weeks. One evening as I visited them, they asked me if I would sit with Joe while they went to have some dinner together as a whole family. They assured me that they would only be gone for about an hour, but they didn't want to leave Joe alone. I was honored to have the privilege to sit with him and released them to go to dinner. As I took his hand, Joe briefly opened his eyes, saw that his pastor was there, smiled, and then slipped back into sleep.

Though sleeping, Joe firmly held my hand. For a while I prayed out loud. Then I read the psalms, particularly Psalms 23, 91, and 103. I then assured him through Scriptures that

God would never leave him alone. I told Joe that my hand in his was to remind him that the Lord and his family were at his side. For a few moments, he labored with his breathing, and then he stepped over from time into eternity. His healing was just as real and dramatic as the healings I have witnessed at the altar and in healing crusades.

Joe had lived in God's purpose and died glorifying God. His family returned. With tears abounding, we all circled Joe's bed and prayed, glorifying God for Joe's life.

Living may be so painful for you or a loved one now that you are praying, like Joe and his family, for God to heal *now* or to release you or them from this life into eternity. Or life may be so purposeful now for you or a loved one that you are praying for God to physically heal *now!* May I invite you to add to the kinds of prayers that you are praying, this kind of prayer—a *magnificat*. Such a prayer glorifies God in all circumstances and seeks His glory in all outcomes. It might be prayed this way:

Father, the God who Heals, I glorify You for healing me eternally by the stripes of Your Only begotten Son, Jesus.
I glorify You, if you heal me now.
I glorify You, if you heal me later.
I glorify You, in my life and in my death.
I glorify You for healing in time and eternally.
I glorify You in everything. Amen.

When God doesn't heal *now*, do this with everything else that you do—*glorify* the Lord with every breath that you take!

NOTES

INTRODUCTION

1. Sinclair B. Ferguson, David F. Wright, J. I. Packer, *The New Dictionary of Theology* (Downers Grove, IL: InterVarsity Press, 1988), 450.

CHAPTER 2

1. Francis Schaeffer, *The Francis A. Schaeffer Trilogy: The 3 Essential Books in 1 Volume (The God Who Is There, Escape from Reason,* and *He Is There and He Is Not Silent* (Wheaton: Crossway, 1990).

2. Paul R. House, *Old Testament Theology* (Downers Grove, IL: InterVarsity Press, 1998), 541.

3. J. N. Scofield, *Introducing Old Testament Theology* (Philadelphia: Westminster Press, 1964), 26.

CHAPTER 3

1. Frederick K. C. Price, *Is Healing for All?* (Tulsa, OK: Harrison House, 1976), 76.

2. Peter Youngren, *A Study of God . . . the Healer* (St. Catharine's World Impact Ministries, Ontario: 1986), 48–50.

3. Oral Roberts, William DeArteaga, Paul Thigpen, and Jack Deere, *Miracles Never Cease* (Lake Mary, FL: Creation House, 1991), 55–56.

4. Kenneth and Gloria Copeland, *Healing Promises* (Fort Worth, TX: Kenneth Copeland Productions, 1994), 161.
5. Frederick K. C. Price, *Is Healing for All?* (Tulsa, OK: Harrison House, 1976), 76.
6. Reginald B. Cherry, *The Bible Cure* (Lake Mary, FL: Creation House, 1998), 45ff.
7. A. B. Simpson, *The Gospel of Healing* (Camp Hill, PA: Christian Publications, 1994), 66–67.
8. Kenneth E. Hagin, *Healing Scriptures* (Tulsa, OK: Faith Library Publications, 1993), 1.
9. 1 John 1:1–14.

CHAPTER 4

1. Simpson, *Gospel of Healing*, 61–62.
2. Price, *Is Healing for All?*, 41–42.
3. Alyce M. McKenzie, *Interpretation Bible Studies: Matthew* (Louisville, KY: Geneva Press, 1998), 59.
4. Letter to Pastor Severin Schulze, Theodore J. Tappert, ed., trans. June 1, 1545, in *Luther: Letters of Spiritual Consel* (London: S.C.M. Press, 1955), 51ff.
5. Becky Tirabassi, *Let Prayer Change Your Life* (Nashville: Thomas Nelson, 1990), 117.
6. Andrew Murray, as quoted in ibid., 147ff.

CHAPTER 5

1. Cherry, *The Bible Cure*, 19ff.
2. M. Basil Pennington, Alan Jones, Mark Booth, eds., *The Living Testament* (San Francisco: Harper & Row, 1985), 90. From the breastplate of Saint Patrick.
3. Simpson, *Gospel of Healing*, 64.
4. Billy Joe Daughtery, *You Can Be Healed* (Tulsa, OK: Harrison House, 1991), 65.

CHAPTER 6

1. Andrew Murray, *Divine Healing* (Washington, PA: Christian Literature Crusade, 1995), 121.

CHAPTER 7

1. Eddie Hyatt, *2000 Years of Charismatic Christianity* (Tulsa, OK: Hyatt International Ministries, 1996).

2. Irenaeus, *Against Heresies*, vol. 1 of *The Anti-Nicene Library*, ed. Rev. Alexander Roberts and James Donaldson (Edinburgh: T&T Clark, 1974), 409.

3. Origen, ibid., vol. 3, 473.

4. Athanasius, *Life of Antony*, ibid., vol. 4, 200.

5. Augustine, *The City of God*, 485ff.

6. Saint Gregory the Great, *Dialogues*, vol. 39 of *The Fathers of the Church*, trans. Odo John Zimmerman (New York: Fathers of the Church, 1959), 76f.

7. Philip Schaff and Henry Wace, eds., *Nicene and Post-Nicene Fathers of the Christian Church*, 2d series, vol. 5, 503f.

8. John Horsch, "The Faith of the Swiss Brethren, II" *Mennonite Quarterly Review* 5, no. 1 (1931).

9. A. J. Gordon, *The Ministry of Healing* (Harrisburg, PA: Christian Publications, 1961), 67.

10. John Wesley, *The Words of John Wesley* vol. 8 (Grand Rapids, MI: Zondervan, n.d.), 465.

11. Gerhard Kittel and Gerhard Friedrich, *Theological Dictionary of the New Testament*, vol. 7, trans. Geoffrey W. Bromiley (Grand Rapids, MI: Eerdmans, 1971), 965ff.

12. Notes from the Barods, India, crusade conducted by Peter Youngren, March 1998.

CHAPTER 8

1. Adapted and quoted from Ferguson, Wright, and Packer, "Sovereignty of God," *The New Dictionary of Theology*, 654ff.

2. John Sanders, *The God Who Risks* (Downers Grove, IL: InterVarsity Press, 1998), 235–36.

3. Ibid., 271.

4. Ibid., 282.

CHAPTER 9

1. Reginald B. Cherry with Larry Keefauver, *The Doctor and the Word* (Lake Mary, FL: Creation House, 1996), 103.

ABOUT THE AUTHOR

LARRY KEEFAUVER, D.Min., is senior editor of *Ministries Today* magazine. He co-pastors The Gathering Place Worship Center in Lake Mary, Florida. He has been a guest on *The 700 Club*, TBN, and the *Family and Marriage Magazine* on Fox.

Dr. Keefauver has written more than forty-five books and curriculum studies, including editing *The Holy Spirit Encounter Bible* and writing the eight accompanying study guides. His most recent books include *Lord, I Wish My Family Would Get Saved; Lord, I Wish My Teenager Would Talk With Me; Lord, I Wish My Husband Would Pray With Me;* and *Hugs for Grandparents.*

Dr. Keefauver and his wife, Judi, frequently lead one-day marriage seminars throughout the United States and internationally. Dr. Keefauver ministers, keynotes, and speaks on healing, the Holy Spirit, and marriage and family. His ministry can be contacted at 1-800-750-5306.